MISSIONAL HOSPITALITY

Study by Judson Edwards
Commentary by Cecil Sherman

Free downloadable Teaching Guide for this study available at
NextSunday.com/teachingguides

NextSunday Resources
6316 Peake Road
Macon, Georgia 31210-3960
1-800-747-3016
©2014 by NextSunday Resources
All rights reserved.

TABLE OF CONTENTS

Missional Hospitality

HOW TO USE THIS STUDY

NextSunday Resources Adult Bible Studies are designed to help adults study Scripture seriously within the context of the larger Christian tradition and, through that process, find their faith renewed, challenged, and strengthened. We study the Scriptures because we believe they affect our current lives in important ways. Each study contains the following three components:

Study Guide

Each study guide lesson is arranged in four movements:

Reflecting recalls a contemporary story, anecdote, example, or illustration to help us anticipate the session's relevance in our lives.

Studying is centered on giving the biblical material in-depth attention while often surrounding it with helpful insights from theology, ethics, church history, and other areas.

Understanding helps us find relevant connections between our lives and the biblical message.

What About Me? provides brief statements that help unite life issues with the meaning of the biblical text.

Commentary

Each study guide lesson is accompanied by an additional, in-depth commentary on the biblical material. Written by a different author than the study guide, each commentary gives the opportunity for learners to approach the Scripture text from a separate but complementary viewpoint.

Teaching Guide

In addition to the provided study guide and commentary, *NextSunday Resources* also provides a *free* downloadable teaching guide, available at NextSunday.com. Each teaching guide gives the teacher tools for focusing on the content of each study guide lesson through additional commentary and Bible background information. Through teacher helps and teaching options, each teaching guide also provides substance for variety and choice in the preparation of each lesson.

NextSunday
Resources

STUDY INTRODUCTION

If we are serious about following Jesus, we will be people of open hearts, open hands, and open homes. In other words, as followers of Jesus we will practice the fine art of hospitality.

In this unit, we will study five facets of Christian hospitality. As we do so, we will be reminded that hospitality is "missional." That is, simply by being hospitable, we will be on mission for Christ.

In the first session, we reflect on a passage from Job, where Job proclaims his lifelong practice of showing hospitality to strangers. This first session highlights hospitality as a central virtue in both the Old and New Testaments.

The second session specifically addresses hospitality to the poor. Our spotlighted passage is from the book of Ruth, where Boaz practically and kindly reaches out to Ruth in her poverty.

The third session focuses on hospitality to sinners. We study the episode in John's Gospel where Jesus forgives the woman caught in the act of adultery and use that passage to consider our own response to sinful people.

The fourth session focuses on hospitality to newcomers, specifically newcomers in our church. The passage we use in this session is from 1 Corinthians 14, where the apostle Paul encourages the Corinthians to consider the needs of others in their times of worship.

We wrap up our study of Christian hospitality by reminding ourselves that all of our hospitality is really hospitality to Christ. The final session in our study focuses on the parable of the sheep and goats in Matthew 25, where Jesus says all of our hospitality is actually done to, and for, him.

The good news about hospitality is that it doesn't require us to have money, education, brilliance, fame, or power. It only requires that we open our hearts, our hands, and our homes to the people around us.

1

HOSPITALITY TO STRANGERS

Job 31:16-23, 31-32

Central Question

What value do I place on hospitality?

Scripture

Job 31:16-23, 31-32 16 "If I have withheld anything that the poor desired, or have caused the eyes of the widow to fail, 17 or have eaten my morsel alone, and the orphan has not eaten from it— 18 for from my youth I reared the orphan like a father, and from my mother's womb I guided the widow— 19 if I have seen anyone perish for lack of clothing, or a poor person without covering, 20 whose loins have not blessed me, and who was not warmed with the fleece of my sheep; 21 if I have raised my hand against the orphan, because I saw I had supporters at the gate; 22 then let my shoulder blade fall from my shoulder, and let my arm be broken from its socket. 23 For I was in terror of calamity from God, and I could not have faced his majesty.... 31 if those of my tent ever said, 'O that we might be sated with his flesh!'— 32 the stranger has not lodged in the street; I have opened my doors to the traveler—...."

Reflecting

Our church has just passed through a wonderful season of hospitality. It started when a couple in our church volunteered to be a host family for the "Samaritan's Purse Children's Heart Project." In this program, children with heart defects from around the world are flown to the United States and given heart surgery in selected hospitals.

That's why 18-month-old Davaa and 17-year-old Zolo, their mothers, and a translator flew into San Antonio from their homes in Mongolia to embark on a special adventure. The host couple in our church had agreed to house, feed, and provide transportation for these Mongolian guests, but the enterprise quickly became a church-wide event. We all realized that two people simply couldn't meet all the needs of these guests from afar.

> The Greek word for hospitality (*philoxenia*) literally means "love of foreigners."

Some church people brought meals to feed them. Others provided transportation to and from doctor's offices and hospitals. After the two boys had successful heart surgeries, our church people surrounded the Mongolians with love and attention. One family bought them all cowboy boots. Another took them to the zoo. Another took them to the rodeo. Two women in our church even took them on a shopping expedition.

Our five Mongolian guests blessed us in return. They came to our worship services on Sunday, ate supper with us on Wednesday nights, and did their best to communicate their gratitude. We were impressed with their resilience, their buoyant spirit, and their willingness to embrace a new culture.

When those five Mongolian people boarded their plane to return home, Davaa and Zolo had repaired hearts, Zolo and the two mothers had chosen to walk the Jesus Way, and our church had learned again the power of hospitality.

Studying

> The parable of the good Samaritan shows us three approaches to life: "What's yours is mine and I'll take it" (the thieves), "What's mine is mine and I'll keep it" (the priest and Levite), and "What's mine is yours and I'll give it" (the good Samaritan).

Tucked away in the book of Job is a passage that extols the virtue of the hospitable life. It's in Job 31, where Job defends himself against the charges of his friends Eliphaz, Bildad, and Zophar. These three friends assumed that suffering was always the result of sin, so they loudly proclaimed that Job must have done something awful to deserve such a miserable fate.

When you read the charges of these friends against Job, you are justified in asking, with friends like these, who needs enemies?

But Job rose from his sackcloth and ashes, summoned his courage, and offered a rousing defense. Included in his defense is the passage about hospitality. It's in the form of an oath that follows a common pattern in Old Testament days: "If I have done any of these things, then let something bad happen to me." In Job's case, it was, "If I have ever failed to show hospitality, let my shoulder blade fall from my shoulder, and let my arm be broken from its socket." That's a serious and graphic oath!

When you read the passage closely, you can pick out the specifics in Job's concept of hospitality. For Job, hospitality involves such activities as taking care of poor people and widows (v. 16), feeding and caring for orphans (vv. 17-18), providing clothes for the needy (vv. 19-20), defending the cause of orphans at "the gate," that is, at the community's center of justice (v. 21), and opening his door and pantry to strangers (vv. 31-32). In Job's mind, his goodness had something to do with how hospitable he had always been to "the least of these" (see Mt 25:31-46). As we will see when we get to the last session in this study, years later Jesus would affirm Job's thinking.

Job's impassioned use of "the hospitality defense" reminds us that hospitality is a central virtue in the Bible. The host-guest relationship involved solemn commitments from both parties. According to Robert Dunston,

> Typically a stranger would enter a city, go to an open place, and wait for an invitation from someone to lodge for the night (Gen 19:1-3; Judg 19:15-21). The one who offered hospitality treated the stranger well. The stranger's animals were cared for, water was provided for him to wash his feet and he was provided with a meal and rest (Gen 18:1-8; 19:1-3; 24:31-33). Protection was also provided for the stranger even if it put the host and his family in peril (Gen 19:6-9; Judg 19:22-24). Hospitality thus went well beyond simply providing for basic needs. Perhaps through such meticulous care, the host hoped to turn aside an enemy's wrath (2 Kgs 6:11-23) or even turn an enemy into a friend (Prov 25:21-22). (393)

In the New Testament as well, hospitality is an important value. It is a central feature in Jesus' parable of the Good Samaritan (Lk 10:25-37). The priest and the Levite passed the wounded man without lifting a finger to help, but the Samaritan was hospitable to him. Unlike the paragons of Jewish virtue, this hated outsider saw the man on the side of the road, bandaged his wounds, put him on a donkey, took him to an inn, and got him through what must have been a long and painful night. Jesus said, "Go and do likewise" (Lk 10:37). That's the ethic of the Jesus Way. His people are typically hospitable.

It's not surprising at all, then, to read Paul telling both Timothy and Titus that church leaders should be hospitable (1 Tim 3:2; Titus 1:8) or to read his counsel to the Roman Christians: "Extend hospitality to strangers" (Rom 12:13). Nor is it surprising to read Peter's advice in 1 Peter 4:9: "Be hospitable to one another without complaining." Then there's the famous line from the writer of the book of Hebrews: "Do not neglect to show hospitality to strangers, for by doing that some have entertained angels without knowing it" (Heb 13:2).

In this unit of study, all those biblical admonitions launch us on a journey toward a truth we often forget: a significant part of following Jesus involves practicing the art of hospitality. Jimmy Carter once said that his life changed when he was asked the question, "If you were on trial for being a Christian, would there be enough evidence to convict you?" (Norton and Slosser, 90). If someone asked us that question, we would probably rise up, Job-like, to speak words in our own defense. We might talk about how often we go to church, how much money we have given to the church, how long we have been married, how long we have held our job, or how we've never once been in trouble with the law. We could probably make an impressive case for our goodness.

> If you were on trial for being a Christian, would there be enough evidence to convict you?

But we would also probably never think of saying one word about hospitality. It's not much on the "radar" anymore—in our minds or in our churches. It just wouldn't cross our minds to say what Job said when he wanted to identify himself: "Look at the way I've been hospitable through the years, and you'll see very clearly who I am."

Understanding

In the introduction to this unit on "Missional Hospitality," I wrote that following Jesus means we are people of open hearts, open hands, and open homes. Though Job lived a long time before Jesus, his defense to his friends was basically that he had always had an open heart, an open hand, and an open home. He opened his heart and hands to poor people, widows, and orphans, and he opened his home to strangers needing food and a place to stay. He rested his case on his hospitality.

As we think of practical and personal applications for this passage from Job, it would behoove us to look at our hearts, our hands, and our homes. Focusing on these three things can provide us a better view of our practice of hospitality.

First, do I have an open heart? The writer of 1 John asks a pointed question: "How does God's love abide in anyone who has the world's good and sees a brother or sister in need and yet refuses to help?" (1 Jn 3:17). Can we still feel pity? Are we regularly moved to tears by the plight of people around us? Do we still have an open, tender heart?

Second, do I have open hands? Will I move beyond pity and compassion and actually do something? Will I move beyond feelings to actions? John goes on to say: "Little children, let us not love in word or speech, but in truth and action" (1 Jn 3:18).

Finally, do I have an open home? Will I use my home as a place where strangers can be refreshed, friendships can be nurtured, and people can find food and rest?

If, like Job, we can point to a life of hospitality, we have the best proof possible of a life led with purpose in close communion with God.

What About Me?

• *Hospitality is the forgotten virtue in today's concept of Christian discipleship.* Christians know they should pray, worship, read the

Bible, and give, but practicing hospitality is not often thought of as one of the necessary Christian disciplines.

• *Hospitality is accessible to anyone.* Any person can make hospitality a priority, regardless of age, race, education, or income. It's an equal-opportunity spiritual discipline.

• *Hospitable people get a double blessing.* Those who practice hospitality not only give a blessing, they receive one as well. As the writer of Hebrews puts it, we often entertain angels without knowing it. The Mongolian people who visited our church are a perfect example.

• *Churches, as well as individuals, can learn to practice hospitality.* Hospitality is the calling not only of persons but also of churches. Churches can house missionaries on furlough, provide shelter for the homeless, make soup for the hungry, and consider other ways to extend the open heart, open hand, and open home.

Resources

Robert C. Dunston, "Hospitality," *Mercer Dictionary of the Bible*, ed. Watson E. Mills et al. (Macon, GA: Mercer University Press, 1990).

Howard Norton & Bob Slosser, *The Miracle of Jimmy Carter* (Plainfield NJ: Logos, 1976).

HOSPITALITY TO STRANGERS

Job 31:16-23, 31-32

Introduction

Hospitality is rarely mentioned at church. For us, hospitality is more a matter of culture and good manners than Christian conduct. People who never attend church are just as likely to be hospitable as we are. This shows that Christian hospitality is really at the margins of what we teach at church. The lessons for the next five Sundays explore the biblical basis for Christian hospitality.

The first lesson comes from the book of Job. That is a part of the Bible most class members will not know well. They know Job had troubles, and popular wisdom says he was "patient." That may be the depth of their knowledge of Job, so consider some background material.

Job is wisdom literature, which is primarily concerned with practical, functional religion and conduct. Our text is sublime both in subject and form; it is great literature. Alfred Lord Tennyson called it "the greatest poem of ancient or modern times" (Ralph Smith, *Job: A Study in Providence and Faith* [Nashville: Convention, 1971] 1). We are dealing with great and inspired literature. But we are also handling poetry that is sometimes difficult to interpret.

Job was a good man, "blameless and upright, one who feared God and turned away from evil" (Job 1:1). It was thought that if you were good, bad things would not come your way. Bad things were seen as divine punishment. Job challenged that theology. He was good and yet a lot of bad things came his way. What did that mean? Was Job only pretending to be good? How can bad things happen to good people?

Our text comes from Job 31. The whole chapter is Job's "oath of innocence." In it he names many acts of wrongdoing to which he pleads innocence. His conscience is clear; he is without blame. Samuel Terrien says of Job 31, "[Job] examines a series of more than sixteen concrete hypotheses of sinful acts, each one beginning with the conjunction 'If'. . . and he clears himself of any deed—or even intention—of religious or ethical turpitude, thereby revealing in exquisite terms the highest moral conscience to be found in the O. T." ("Job," *The Interpreter's Bible*, vol. 3 [Nashville: Abingdon, 1954] 1117).

The culture from which Job is written is different from ours; that will be noted below. But so noble and true are Job's standards that they are pressed forward to our time. They are not just ancient, Middle Eastern norms that we study like historical sociologists. God is looking for the same high standards in us.

I. Job's Lifelong Pattern of Hospitality

Job's friends had a wooden, brittle theology that said bad things come upon people who are bad. From that premise they reasoned that, since Job had had all sorts of calamities come upon him, Job had been bad. His terrible run of misfortune was a result of his sins.

One of Job's "comforters," Eliphaz the Temanite, accused him of a lack of hospitality: "You have given no water to the weary to drink, and you have withheld bread from the hungry. . . . You have sent widows away empty-handed, and the arms of the orphans you have crushed" (Job 22:7, 9). If what Eliphaz said was true, it could be argued that Job's extreme misfortune was a result of his self-centeredness.

Job would have none of their "tit-for-tat" theology. He knew how he had lived, and he was not willing to be silent before their accusations. All of Job 31 is a series of justifications. Sixteen times he poses hypothetical questions. Our text involves the three questions that speak to Job's willingness to practice hospitality.

• "If I have withheld anything that the poor desired. . . " (31:16a).
• "If I have seen anyone perish for lack of clothing, or a poor person without covering. . . " (31:19).
• If I have raised my hand against the orphan. . . " (31:21).

In each instance Job made the case that he was not guilty of neglecting even strangers who needed him. To the contrary, he had gone out of his way throughout his life to make provision for them. He had done what he was supposed to do. So Job defended his lifelong pattern of hospitality. He said,

• "From my youth I reared the orphan like a father, and from my mother's womb I guided the widow" (31:18).
• Poor people were "warmed with the fleece of my sheep" (31:20b).
• If I have ever neglected the orphan, "let my shoulder blade fall from my shoulder, and let my arm be broken from its socket" (31:22).

What Job did was part of the culture of the Middle East. As V. H. Koon explains, "Public inns were a rarity and every stranger a potential enemy. Hospitality was discharged more from fear and for protection than from generosity.... Moreover, the host never knew when he himself would be dependent on others" ("Hospitality," *The Interpreter's Dictionary of the Bible*, vol. 2 [Nashville: Abindgon, 1962] 654). A Bible illustration of ancient hospitality comes from Abraham's nephew, Lot, who entertained the mysterious guests at his home in Sodom (Gen 19:1-3). Had the strangers not come under Lot's care, they would have been prey for dangerous street people (19:4-11). For another illustration of Old Testament hospitality, see Judges 19:15-21.

Hospitality was not given in a stingy fashion. Provision for animals, water for feet, rest for the body, and a large meal were all part of ancient hospitality. Job argued that he did all of this, and not only as an occasional burst of generosity. Rather, it was the pattern of his life.

II. Job's Reason for Hospitality

Koon said the reason for ancient hospitality was self-interest. If strangers were not taken in, they were likely to become a danger. That may have been so for most people, but Job worked from higher motivations. He tells us why he helped strangers and took care of widows and orphans: "For I was in terror of calamity from

God and I could not have faced his majesty" (31:23). Job did what he did because he believed God expected him to be hospitable. He could not bear the thought of standing before God at judgment and having to give an account of why he had not welcomed the stranger, cared for the widow, fed the orphan, clothed those who were naked.

Job lived before the time of Jesus, but in some ways he had a clearer picture of the nature of God than present-day Christians. Religion is constantly shaping us. We are being molded to the pattern of our understanding of the nature of God. If we believe God cares for the needy, then eventually we will care for them, too. We take on the nature of the God we worship. The sense of the Old Testament is that God welcomed strangers and wanted his people to do the same. Job was trying to act as his God did. This idea of building our conduct around our understanding of the nature of God raises the question of what the average church member thinks about God and hospitality.

There is cause to be hopeful about the answer to that question. A hundred years ago, most of our churches were preaching a gospel that paid little attention to the plight of those in need of help. Salvation for the soul was the only message. The care of the body and a tender heart for needy strangers were not being preached. There was hospitality, but it was usually confined to kin and close friends. Then a Baptist teacher-preacher named Walter Rauschenbusch began arguing that Jesus cared for the poor. His arguments were persuasive because they were biblically based. Critics called his message a "Social Gospel," but what he said fit what Jesus did. Jesus fed people. He healed them. He cared for them. Rauschenbusch argued that if the ways and words of Jesus were really the standard for the church for all time, then the church needed to broaden its message and shape itself into an institution that cared for others as well as an evangelistic enterprise.

Not all the church welcomed the Social Gospel, but even those parts of the church that resisted have been influenced by it. Mission boards no longer send only evangelists; now they send doctors, educators, and agricultural missionaries. The reason for the change is not Walter Rauschenbusch. He was simply the one who sounded the alarm that the church had diminished the gospel of Jesus. The real power for change came because Christians began to pay attention to parts of the Bible we had previously overlooked.

In Jesus' parable of the sheep and the goats (Mt 25:31-46), the basis for our judgment is the way we have shown hospitality to those in need. We will discuss this familiar passage in the last lesson of this unit, but its central message runs through all of these lessons. God welcomed into heaven those who were hospitable to strangers, the poor, and others in need, but condemned those who had neglected them, asserting, "Truly I tell you, just as you did not do it to one of the least of these, you did not do it to me" (Mt 25:44-45). We care for people in need because Jesus did, and we are trying to reshape our lives to the standard of Jesus. Job figured this out before Jesus lived on earth. He cared for needy people because he believed God cared for needy people.

III. Getting from Theology to Practice

Preaching the gospel is easier than practicing the gospel. Everybody knows Christians are supposed to care for those who need our help. A poor stranger sat in my office in Asheville, North Carolina, and said, "You have to give me money; the Bible says you are supposed to." And he was right (see Matt 5:42). We are to be generous, but how do we do it? We don't live in the ancient Near East. The way Job practiced hospitality is not the way I am supposed to. If we take derelicts into our homes, we may be robbed or hurt. I don't do it. That does not excuse me from the obligation to help others. I have to find another way to do it that is practical in our culture.

I don't have all the answers, but here are some suggestions that make sense to me.

(1) Most cities have established food banks to which people of means (that's us) bring food that is then distributed to the hungry. Often food banks ask for money from us. They use that money to buy large quantities of food at reduced prices in order to share it with those who need it.

(2) In Fort Worth, Presbyterians developed a ministry they called "The Presbyterian Night Shelter." But it was funded by every part of the Christian community. Broadway Baptist Church gave money and time to the ministry, and so did Methodists, Disciples, Lutherans, Catholics, and others. Dinner was served to anyone at night; breakfast was served in the morning, and a few staff and many volunteers helped enforce the rules. This was hospitality offered in the name of Jesus: a contemporary way of caring for the hungry.

(3) Church budgets that once set aside next to nothing for the needy now include them. A small church can do a little; a big church can do a lot. Often these churches combine their resources. A Methodist pastor in Asheville, North Carolina, dreamed up a way to pull a lot of churches into a ministry for those in need. He called it "Asheville and Buncombe Cooperative Christian Ministries." Numerous churches support it both with money and volunteers.

These are only a few of the ways churches can take this lesson to heart. It is certainly easier to help people we know. But there's a way to help others who may be strangers to us, if there is a will to do it. We must remember that no one is a stranger to God.

Job comes out of the Old Testament; he did not have the full revelation of God that we have in Jesus. But in that long-ago day, Job still saw the face of God clearly. God knows and loves everyone individually. We aren't able to know everyone in that way, but we can strive to see them as God sees them—people created in God's image. When we do, we can't help but care for them by showing Christian hospitality.

Notes

Notes

HOSPITALITY TO THE POOR

Ruth 2:2-17

Central Question

What can I do for poor people in my community?

Scripture

Ruth 2:2-17 2 And Ruth the Moabite said to Naomi, "Let me go to the field and glean among the ears of grain, behind someone in whose sight I may find favor." She said to her, "Go, my daughter." 3 So she went. She came and gleaned in the field behind the reapers. As it happened, she came to the part of the field belonging to Boaz, who was of the family of Elimelech. 4 Just then Boaz came from Bethlehem. He said to the reapers, "The LORD be with you." They answered, "The LORD bless you." 5 Then Boaz said to his servant who was in charge of the reapers, "To whom does this young woman belong?" 6 The servant who was in charge of the reapers answered, "She is the Moabite who came back with Naomi from the country of Moab. 7 She said, 'Please, let me glean and gather among the sheaves behind the reapers.' So she came, and she has been on her feet from early this morning until now, without resting even for a moment." 8 Then Boaz said to Ruth, "Now listen, my daughter, do not go to glean in another field or leave this one, but keep close to my young women. 9 Keep your eyes on the field that is being reaped, and follow behind them. I have ordered the young men not to bother you. If you get thirsty, go to the vessels and drink from what the young men have drawn." 10 Then she fell prostrate, with her face to he ground, and said to him, "Why have I found favor in your sight, that you should take notice of me, when I am a foreigner?" 11 But Boaz answered her, "All that you have done for your mother-in-law since the death of your husband has been fully told me, and how you left your father and mother and your native land and came to a people that you did not know before. 12 May the LORD reward you for your deeds, and may you have a full reward from the LORD, the God of Israel, under whose wings you have come for refuge!" 13 Then she said, "May I continue to find favor in your sight, my lord, for you have comforted me and spoken kindly to your servant, even though I am not one of your servants." 14 At mealtime Boaz said to her, "Come here, and eat some of this bread, and dip your morsel in the sour wine." So she sat beside the reapers, and he heaped up for her some parched grain. She ate until she was satisfied, and she had some left over. 15 When she got up to glean, Boaz instructed his young men, "Let her glean even among the standing sheaves, and do not reproach her. 16 You must also pull out some handfuls for her from the bundles, and leave them for her to glean, and do not rebuke her." 17 So she gleaned in the field until evening. Then she beat out what she had gleaned, and it was about an ephah of barley.

Reflecting

Last week, as we began our study of missional hospitality, we saw that being hospitable means we have open hearts, open hands, and open homes. Perhaps we should add a fourth characteristic to the list. We also need to have open eyes.

When the writer of 1 John asks, "How does God's love abide in anyone who has the world's goods and sees a brother or sister in need and yet refuses to help?" (1 Jn 3:17), he assumes that the person sees that brother or sister in need. But what if that doesn't happen? What if we don't see? What if our eyes are closed, and we neglect that brother or sister—not because we don't care, but simply because we don't see?

> **?** When did you last see a poor person and do something tangible to help him or her?

Our session this week zeroes in on hospitality to the poor. The place to begin the session is simply by asking ourselves if we ever see any poor people. If we live in middle- or upper-class

2

America, we likely never lay eyes on poor people. We might occasionally see a beggar downtown or someone standing on a street corner asking for a handout, but we don't actually know anyone who is hungry, thirsty, homeless, or desperate. Poverty lives a long way from us. It's not that we're callous and unkind; we simply don't see the needs.

And until we open our eyes and start to see them, we'll never show hospitality to the poor.

Studying

Our passage from the book of Ruth gives us an example of a wealthy person who opened his eyes and helped someone who was poor. Boaz, "a prominent rich man" (2:1), saw Ruth in his field gleaning ears of grain, and had mercy on her. He went out of his way to help her and give her dignity.

The whole idea of "gleaning" is foreign to many of us. In Leviticus 19:9-10, God spells out the principle of gleaning:

> When you reap the harvest of your land, you shall not reap to the very edges of your field, or gather the gleanings of your harvest. You shall not strip your vineyard bare, or gather the fallen grapes of your vineyard; you shall leave them for the poor and the alien; I am the LORD your God.

Some of the crop was to be left for the poor and the alien. Landowners were not to strip the fields bare, but instead they were to leave some "gleanings" for those who could come along behind them and find enough food to stave off starvation. Other Old Testament passages indicate the gleanings were for the poor, the alien, the widow, and the orphan. These vulnerable people were taken care of by the gleanings in the field.

That's what Ruth was doing in Boaz's field. She was gathering the gleanings so that she and her mother-in-law, Naomi, could eat. Ruth fit into three of the four categories I just listed. She was poor, an alien (from the land of Moab), and a widow. She was a prime candidate for the gleanings.

Boaz saw her in the field and inquired about her. His people told him all about Ruth, that she had requested to glean the

fields, and that she had been on her feet all day without any rest. Boaz's response to her went above and beyond the call of duty or the letter of the law. He saw her situation, assessed her need, and did four gracious things on her behalf.

First, he encouraged her to stay only in his field and not to glean in any others. This statement reveals his care and concern.

Second, he told her to stay close to the other women in the field. For her own protection, Ruth was not to wander off by herself.

Third, he warned the young men in the field not to bother her. As a young, alien widow, Ruth would have been fair game for any unscrupulous man, so Boaz issued a warning on her behalf.

Fourth, Boaz invited Ruth to drink the water that was available for his workers. This was a special privilege not typically offered to strangers.

Ruth immediately realized that she had been the recipient of special treatment and "fell prostrate, with her face to the ground, and said to him, 'Why have I found favor in your sight, that you should take notice of me, when I am a foreigner?'" (v. 10).

Boaz replied that he knew of her past and her faithfulness to her mother-in-law, and then he did two more gracious deeds for her. First, he invited her to eat bread and drink wine with the workers. Then Boaz instructed his men to "let her glean among the standing sheaves, and do not reproach her" (v. 15). In other words, she was to have access to the "first fruits," not just the leftovers. Boaz evidently wanted to make sure that Ruth got plenty of food for her and Naomi.

To read further from the Old Testament about taking care of the poor, read Jeremiah 5:27-29 and Micah 3:5.

The story continues: "So she gleaned in the field until evening. Then she beat out what she had gleaned, and it was about an ephah of barley" (v. 17). An ephah of barley was about 42 quarts and would feed two people for nearly a week. After her time in Boaz's field, Ruth was secure, at least for a while. She and Naomi had plenty to eat, and it was all because Boaz saw her and went out of his way to be hospitable to her.

Boaz's gracious treatment of Ruth was supposed to be the norm in the Old Testament, but the people of Israel often forgot to be hospitable to the poor. The prophets had to keep reminding them of their responsibility. These verses from Isaiah are typical of the prophets' teachings about the sort of "fast" that is acceptable to God:

> Is it not to share your bread with the hungry, and bring the homeless poor into your house, when you see the naked, to cover them, and not to hide yourself from your own kin?. . . if you offer your food to the hungry and satisfy the needs of the afflicted, then your light shall rise in the darkness and your gloom be like the noonday. (Isa 58:7, 10)

Israel's future would be bright if only they remembered to take care of the poor the way Boaz took care of Ruth.

Understanding

Our problem is that, unlike Boaz, we don't usually see the Ruths around us. We're isolated and insulated from the poor. What

can we do to practice hospitality to poor people? How can we minister to people we don't usually see?

The answer to those questions is actually simple. We go where poor people are. We get out of our middle- or upper-class culture from time to time and step into the lower-class culture. We walk out into the field and actively seek out Ruth.

Our church is a middle-class congregation in the suburbs of San Antonio. I don't know of one person in our church who is hungry or homeless. As far as I know, we all eat well, drive more-than-adequate cars, and sleep in air-conditioned houses. Our church has never even thought of beginning a food pantry, literacy class, or soup kitchen. Cozy in our comfortable cocoons, we would never see Ruth unless we went looking for her. Therefore, on a regular basis, we do.

Several times a year, a group from our church takes food and serves it to the homeless under the Nolan Street Bridge in downtown San Antonio. Alcoholics, drug addicts, and destitute folks line up to eat our food, and we get to see the poor face to face.

Then every summer, a group from our church goes to Guatemala to work in an orphanage for young girls. We hold a Vacation Bible School there and get to see girls in a world very different from ours.

Another group from our church goes to the Texas Valley every summer to do construction on a church there, to hold another Vacation Bible School, and to visit "the colonias," makeshift homes where thousands of people newly arrived from Mexico live. It's culture shock for us when we go, for we rub shoulders with poor people all day long.

We've also built two houses with Habitat for Humanity, our people working side by side with poor families to reach a common goal: good, affordable housing for people who need it.

Like most churches, we have to make ourselves do those things. Left to our own devices, we'd stay comfortable in our nice little cocoon. But we know we're under orders to be hospitable to the poor. And we know we'll never do that unless we leave our "comfort zone" and go looking for poor people.

> **?** Are there poor people in your area whom God is calling your church to serve?

What About Me?

• *We will never see Ruth until we open our eyes.* Most of us tend to be self-absorbed, concerned primarily about "me and mine." Somehow, we have to get our eyes off of ourselves.

• *It is possible that poverty is closer to us than we realize.* Some people in our neighborhood, school, office, or church have more material needs than we realize. We can't assume poverty is only in other places.

• *We have an individual calling to practice hospitality to the poor.* The calling to take care of the poor is for each of us. We each have to craft a personal response to poverty.

• *We also have a corporate calling to practice hospitality to the poor.* Our churches have to look for ways to minister to the poor. Some churches, situated in the midst of poverty, will invite the poor to come to them. Others churches, situated in the midst of luxury, will have to go to the poor.

• *Poor people have a lot to teach the rich.* If we go among the poor, thinking we are the givers and they are the receivers, we are in for a surprise. The joy and simplicity some poor people have will teach us much about what really matters.

HOSPITALITY TO THE POOR

Ruth 2:2-17

Introduction

Even many casual church attenders recognize one quotation from the book of Ruth. In the King James translation, that familiar passage reads like this:

> Entreat me not to leave thee, or to return from following after thee: for whither thou goest, I will go; and where thou lodgest, I will lodge: thy people shall be my people, and thy God my God: Where thou diest, I will die, and there will I be buried; the Lord do so to me, and more also, if ought but death part thee and me. (Ruth 1:16-17)

It is a beautiful statement of unusual loyalty, often read at weddings. But most people haven't a clue what situation prompted the statement or who said it. Here is a little background on Ruth.

First, we don't know who the author is. Tradition ascribed the book to Samuel, but that seems unlikely. The story is true, but it most likely evolved. First it was a story that was passed along by word of mouth from one generation to the next. Later, it was written down. Whoever wrote it was a master with words. It is a lovely story told in superb style. Richard Moulton said the book of Ruth is "so delicate in its transparent simplicity that the worst service one can do the story is to comment on it" ("Ruth," *The Interpreter's Dictionary of the Bible*, vol. 4 [Nashville: Abingdon, 1962] 133). It is my assignment to comment on the story, but Moulton's sentiments are well taken.

The setting for the story is the time of the Judges, circa 1350–1150 BC (Ruth 1:1). Ruth is placed in our Bibles between Judges and Samuel. Both of those books tell of political violence and intrigue, but Ruth is different: the focus here is on the fortunes of a single family.

Two themes are woven throughout the story: the pitiful state of the poor and the providence of God. God would not let Naomi and Ruth starve or be reduced to a meaningless existence. God found a way to provide for their daily needs, and God made a place for them in Israel's history. Ruth was King David's great-grandmother as a result of her marriage to Boaz; being a part of David's genealogy gave her a place in the history of Israel.

Around the edges of this story is a message about Israel's exclusiveness. Strong elements in Jewish life wanted to tighten the boundaries around the people of God. What place should foreigners have in Israel? Did God really welcome converts? How broad were God's sympathies toward Gentiles? The book of Ruth is a soft argument for inclusiveness. I use the word "soft" because Ruth is not an argumentative text. It is lovely, beautiful, almost pastoral. No hint of controversy appears in the text. But in the controversy that raged in Judaism after the Babylonian exile, the story of Ruth came down on the side of inclusiveness.

I. The Plot of the Story

In the days of the Judges, there lived in Bethlehem a man named Elimelech who was married to a woman named Naomi. Famine came upon the land. To survive, Elimelech took his wife and their two sons to Moab. While there, the two sons married Moabite women; one of them married Ruth.

It was not long before Elimelech and both his sons died. Naomi decided to return to her people in Israel. Her daughters-in-law joined her even though they were Moabites. Naomi encouraged them to stay in Moab. Orpah did, but Ruth was uncommonly loyal to Naomi. She would not break ties with her, promising, "Where you go, I will go."

In due time, Naomi and Ruth arrived back in Bethlehem. They had no way to support themselves, so they were reduced to begging. Because of their desperate situation, Ruth went into the field to glean.

Gleaning was not just a social custom; it was supported by Mosaic Law (Lev 19:9; 23:22; Deut 24:19). It was one of the ways

Israelites took care of their poor. The young men who harvested did not do a thorough job. Instead, they left some of the grain in the corners of the fields. Those fragments were available to people who followed behind the harvesters to find something to eat in the leftovers.

While Ruth was gleaning, she "happened" to come to Boaz's field (2:3). Note the subtle way the writer interjects God into the plot. God was at work for good with Naomi and Ruth, and at just the right moment Boaz came from Bethlehem. He immediately noticed Ruth. He asked who the young woman was, and the plot began to thicken.

Boaz is pictured as a wonderful man. He instructed his overseer to protect the Moabite woman from any advances the harvesters might make toward her. She was to be given privileges most gleaners would not get. The harvesters were to leave extra grain for her. Why did Boaz do this? Was his concern for Ruth compassion for the poor? Boaz was related to Naomi. Was his care of Ruth an extension of his kinship to Naomi? Was his generosity an expression of his romantic interest in Ruth? Was Boaz simply a good man who intended to do the right thing no matter what? Was Boaz doing what he did from religious motivations?

I suspect all of the above were a part of his motivations. Every insight into the character of Boaz reveals goodness, and Ruth's beauty, diligence, and loyalty to Naomi obviously made her attractive. Later in the story Boaz went out of his way to ensure that Ruth would not "get away." Boaz bought the field that had once belonged to Elimelech, Naomi's deceased husband. He married Ruth, and they had a son named Obed. Obed was the father of Jesse, who was the father of David. Ruth, the Moabite, became the great-grandmother of the greatest Israelite king.

II. Lessons in the Text

There are many lovely stories in Hebrew history. Why did this one make it into the Bible? What is the story telling us? Specifically, what is Ruth 2:2-17 saying?

God is not put off by foreignness. I was surprised by how many times the book of Ruth mentions that she was a foreigner. The text seems to take every opportunity to remind us Ruth was not an Israelite. The author is whispering something to us (see Ruth 1:22; 2:2, 6, 10, 21; 4:5, 10. The author of Ruth did not think God was bothered or disturbed that Ruth was not an Israelite. God reached out and deliberately made room for Ruth in Israel.

There is a lively debate in our country about immigration. As I write, no resolution has been made of the issue. There are good reasons for this country to set limits on the number who can live here, but there are also good reasons to leave the door open. Nearly all who read these lessons came to America from somewhere else. Our ancestors came from Scotland, England, the Netherlands, Germany, or Italy. Alongside us are people whose ancestors were forced to come as slaves. We are all God's children. God does not notice borders set by people who draw lines on maps. There may come a day when there is not enough water in Southern California to admit any more people, or perhaps the financial burden of social services to the poor will close the border to Mexicans in South Texas. But there is no biblical reason to close the door to the foreigner. Our Bible describes a God who is over all nations and loves all peoples.

God notices the plight of the poor. There were no social services in ancient Israel. Instead of Social Security, disability insurance, or welfare, they had religious laws that made a way for poor people to survive. The laws described in Leviticus 19 and Deuteronomy 24 established the practice of gleaning to see that poor people had enough to eat. When Boaz made space and provision for Ruth and Naomi, he was not merely acting out of romantic interest in Ruth—though that may have been present. He was also doing what the Law of Moses said he was supposed to do.

Part of this story is the plight of the poor in ancient Israel. When Naomi and Ruth came to Bethlehem, neither had land, a husband, or the prospect of food. Before, Naomi and Elimelech had land and a place in the community. When she came back there was nothing.

Boaz acted for God when he welcomed Ruth. He went out of his way to give her food. His religion taught him that people with plenty are obligated to act for God and share with those who have little. I'm not sure our churches are teaching this idea.

John the Baptist said, "Whoever has two coats must share with anyone who has none; and whoever has food must do likewise" (Lk 3:11). Jesus said to feed the hungry, clothe the naked, visit the sick (Mt 25:31-46). The early church wanted leaders who were "hospitable" (1 Tim 3:2). If the Bible informs our conduct, we ought to emphasize care of the poor.

Ruth was not lazy, as Boaz's overseer could attest (2:7). She also commended herself in that she did not abandon the older Naomi. Boaz noticed that Ruth had "left [her] father and mother and [her] native land and came to a people that [she] did not know before" (2:12-13). Therefore, he blessed her in the name of the Lord, "under whose wings you have come for refuge!" Ruth had chosen the God of Israel (1:16). Israel's God made a place for her.

God's providence is under and around all the parts of the story. Sometimes the Bible writers say as much by implication as they say specifically. When the text says, "She came and gleaned in the field behind the reapers. As it happened, she came to the part of the field belonging to Boaz, who was of the family of Elimelech" (2:3), it is telling us about the author's faith in the providence of God. "As it happened" is not an accident; it was the way God arranged things for Ruth. An unseen hand put Ruth in the right place at the right time. A gentle providence made Boaz notice Ruth and have the impulse to care for her, to draw near to her, and finally to love her. God was looking out for Ruth. The good fortune that came to her (and Naomi) was not just happenstance; it was the arrangement of a providing heavenly Father.

Nothing has changed. God still takes care of the faithful. As I reflect on a lifetime that now spans eighty years, I see the providence of God all along the way. There was that day when I walked into Dr. J. M. Price's office at Southwestern Seminary in December 1950. There sat the prettiest girl. She was charming, and I was smitten. Three years later we were married. For me, that was an "as it happened" moment. What seemed chance at the time, I now call God's arrangement. Likewise, God took Ruth by the hand and led her through hard times to a soft landing. God made provision for his own.

Of course one part of this lesson is about the hospitality of Boaz toward Ruth and Naomi. But the larger lesson is about God's hospitality to everyone. The entire book of Ruth is about the way God did not let a poor Israelite and her foreign daughter-in-law get pushed into the trash heap of history. God was the hospitable one, the arranger of events, and the provider of life's necessities. God's character has not changed. God takes care of us. Since we believe we are children of God, we need to depend on the God who did not fail Ruth and will also not fail us.

Notes

Notes

3

HOSPITALITY TO SINNERS

John 7:53–8:11

Central Question

Does self-righteousness keep me from reaching out to others?

Scripture

John 7:53–8:11 7:53 Then each of them went home, 8:1 while Jesus went to the Mount of Olives. 2 Early in the morning he came again to the temple. All the people came to him and he sat down and began to teach them. 3 The scribes and the Pharisees brought a woman who had been caught in adultery; and making her stand before all of them, 4 they said to him, "Teacher, this woman was caught in the very act of committing adultery. 5 Now in the law Moses commanded us to stone such women. Now what do you say?" 6 They said this to test him, so that they might have some charge to bring against him. Jesus bent down and wrote with his finger on the ground. 7 When they kept on questioning him, he straightened up and said to them, "Let anyone among you who is without sin be the first to throw a stone at her." 8 And once again he bent down and wrote on the ground. 9 When they heard it, they went away, one by one, beginning with the elders; and Jesus was left alone with the woman standing before him. 10 Jesus straightened up and said to her, "Woman, where are they? Has no one condemned you?" 11 She said, "No one, sir." And Jesus said, "Neither do I condemn you. Go your way, and from now on do not sin again."

Reflecting

Some situations are easy to assess. When you walk by the principal's office at the high school and see the principal, a middle-aged woman who looks like a teacher, and a long-haired teenager with a surly expression huddled in earnest discussion, it's easy to surmise what's happening. The teenager is a troublemaker brought to the principal by the teacher whose class he has disrupted. The principal must arbitrate this dispute and give the troublemaker his just punishment. But it's easy to guess who is wearing the white hats and who is wearing the dark hat in that room.

It must have been this way, too, in the encounter between Jesus, the scribes and Pharisees, and the woman caught in the act of adultery. Even a casual observer could have assigned the proper roles in that setting: the accused, the accusers, and the arbitrator. And it was easy to see that the woman was wearing the dark hat and the scribes and Pharisees were wearing the white hats. She was the sinner caught in the act of sinning, and they were the protectors of God and God's way.

But when Jesus looked at those people and assessed the situation, he came up with a different evaluation. He determined that things weren't as black and white as they seemed. His evaluation of the situation gives us a new perspective as we relate to the people around us. Jesus reminds us to be careful before we flippantly decide who is wearing which hat.

Studying

Perhaps the best way to explore this passage is to focus specifically on the characters in the encounter: the accused, the accusers, and the arbitrator.

The Accused. The unnamed woman who was brought before Jesus was both guilty and defenseless. She was guilty because she had been caught red-handed in the act of adultery. She was defenseless because the Old Testament Law clearly spelled out what should happen to her: "If a man commits adultery with the wife of his neighbor, both the adulterer and the adulteress shall be put to death" (Lev 20:10). This woman was in deep trouble. Her guilt was clear, and the Law was clear. She was an adulteress, and those who were guilty of adultery had to die for their sin. Her only hope was that someone would offer her grace.

The Accusers. The scribes and Pharisees would certainly not be the ones to offer grace. Their job was to make sure the Law was upheld, and this woman had most assuredly violated the Law. Actually, the case was clear-cut; they had no need of an arbitrator to decide the matter. The only reason they brought her before Jesus was to trap him by putting him in a lose-lose situation.

If Jesus said she was guilty and needed to die, he would lose forever his reputation as a "friend of sinners" (see Mt 11:19). But if he offered her freedom and forgiveness, he would lose forever his reputation as a reputable teacher of the Law. He could be cast as "soft" on adultery and "soft" on the Law. The scribes and Pharisees were trying to paint Jesus into a corner. Whatever he decided, he would lose.

The Arbitrator. There was Jesus in the lose-lose situation his opponents set up for him, called upon to make a decision that would affect this woman's destiny. As you read John's description of Jesus' response to the charges brought against her, several things stand out.

• *Jesus stooped to write something in the dirt.* Exactly what he wrote in the dirt is not told, and there has been much speculation about what he wrote and why he wrote it. Maybe he was buying time, so he could think a while before he responded. Maybe he was trying to get the scribes and Pharisees to repeat their charges so they could see how cruel they sounded. Maybe he was embarrassed by these religious leaders and the shame of the woman and wanted to hide his face from them. Maybe he wrote in the dirt some of the sins of these scribes and Pharisees, shaming them and enabling them to see their own guilt. We'll never know exactly what and why Jesus stooped to write.

• *Jesus saw the woman as a person and not a court case.* The scribes and Pharisees saw this woman as one who had broken the Law. She was guilty, and she deserved to die. Jesus, though, saw her as a person, as someone with a name, a family, a home, and a future. He related to her personally, not legally.

• *Jesus didn't assign the "hats" the way everyone else did.* Contrary to what the casual observer would have seen in this episode, Jesus saw that this woman was capable of good, and the pious religious leaders were capable of wrongdoing. When Jesus stood up from writing in the dirt, he said, "Let anyone among you who is without sin be the first to throw a stone at her" (8:7). He was implying that there was more than one dark hat in that crowd. Jesus refused to see the woman as the villain and the religious leaders as the heroes.

• *Jesus practiced hospitality to the woman.* Though this woman was guilty of adultery, Jesus did a couple of kind things for her (8:11). First, he offered her grace, saying, "Neither do I condemn you." Second, he offered her a challenge: "Go your way, and from now on do not sin again." His words said two important things to that woman: that her past could be forgiven and that her future could be different.

> Indeed, God did not send the Son into the world to condemn the world, but in order that the world might be saved through him. (Jn 3:17)
>
> I do not judge anyone who hears my words and does not keep them, for I came not to judge the world, but to save the world. (Jn 12:47)

By the end of the encounter, the dynamics in the group had changed completely. The woman—the accused—was forgiven of her sin and challenged to change her life. Thanks to the wisdom and kindness of Jesus, she had a life to change! At the same time, the scribes and Pharisees—the accusers—were subtly accused and dropped their rocks and their charges.

And Jesus—the arbitrator—had, at least for the moment, escaped the snare his opponents set for him. He did not downplay the Law, but he maintained his reputation as the gracious friend of sinners.

Understanding

This text reminds us how we are to relate to people who are sinners. The mistake we could make in interpreting this passage is to focus only on Jesus' treatment of the woman, assuming (as

most would) that she is the sinner in the story. But, as Jesus makes clear, she is most definitely not the only sinner in the story. The scribes and Pharisees are sinners, too. Hers is the more obvious sin of adultery. Theirs are the more subtle sins of legalism and judgmentalism.

The episode is full of reminders of how to be hospitable to people who "fall short of the glory of God" (Rom 3:23), but three truths stand out.

First, we need to erase the line between sinners and saints. That's one of the key things Jesus did, and it affected how he treated both the woman and the religious leaders. By seeing the woman as created in the image of God, he affirmed her and gave her a future. By seeing the pious religious leaders as capable of sin and evil, he gave them a moment of self-revelation that could have opened up new futures for them as well. He erased the line between "the good people" and "the bad people" and saw all people as sinners in need of grace and change. If we can erase the line between sinners and saints, we will see ourselves as sinners, too, and not be tempted to throw stones.

Second, we need to see people as persons, not categories. The scribes and Pharisees saw this woman as an adulterer; Jesus saw her as a woman with a name and a personal history. It's all too easy to lump people into categories and treat them as teenagers, fundamentalists, Republicans, Catholics, alcoholics, or any of a million other labels. We show hospitality to sinners by seeing people as individuals and giving them our undivided attention.

Third, we need to balance grace and challenge. Jesus offered the woman a liberating word of grace, but he also gave her a stirring word of challenge. "Neither do I condemn you. Go your way, and from now on do not sin again" was the perfect balance of grace and challenge. His response to the religious leaders struck that balance, too. The trick is not to err too much on either side. As imperfect, sinful people who relate to imperfect, sinful people, we gradually learn how to inject both of those realities into our relationships.

What About Me?

• *What is Jesus saying to me about my sin?* Our sin could be one of the more obvious ones, like the woman's adultery. Or it could be one of the more subtle ones, like the religious leaders' legalism and judgmentalism. How would Jesus assess me?

• *How can I learn to see my sin?* One of the real miracles in this text is that the religious leaders had an "aha!" moment. They saw themselves as they truly were and dropped their stones. It is easy to see the sins of others, but often hard to see our own.

• *How can I gently lead others to see their sins?* We realize the genius of Jesus' relational skills when we think about our own encounters with sinners. Inevitably, we come across as condescending and judgmental and alienate people when we don't intend to. Jesus' model of grace and challenge gives us a goal toward which to aim.

• *What does it say about me if I'm always throwing stones?* One of the more prevalent myths is that criticizing people changes them. If we're always in a critical, stone-throwing mode, it shows we know little about motivating others—and little about the grace-full way of Jesus.

Resources

Raymond E. Brown, *The Gospel according to John*, vol. 1, The Anchor Bible (Garden City NY: Doubleday, 1966).

HOSPITALITY TO SINNERS

John 7:53–8:11

Introduction

Our text is not included in most of the oldest manuscripts, and no serious authority disputes that it is a later insertion into the Gospel of John. The style of this story is not like John's Gospel in vocabulary or grammar. It is more like Luke than John, and some old manuscripts even have this text after Luke 21:38.

We know the story is very old. Papias told a similar story in the second century. Ambrose and Augustine knew the story and commented on it. Jerome knew the story and put it in his Latin Vulgate Bible.

Is this text Scripture? Yes, it is. According to Raymond Brown, "From the standpoint of internal criticism, the story is quite plausible and quite like some of the other gospel stories of attempts to trap Jesus (Luke 20:20, 27). There is nothing in the story itself or its language that would forbid us to think of it as an early story concerning Jesus" (*The Gospel According to John*, vol. 1 [New York: Doubleday, 1966] 335).

Our text is about a woman "caught in adultery" (8:3). She was dragged before Jesus by "the scribes and Pharisees," who wanted Jesus to pass judgment on her and make a public example of her. In fact, the plot of our story is darker and thicker than it appears. Here is some background that influences the way we interpret it.

Adultery was a serious crime in Jewish law. Barclay quotes the rabbis: "Every Jew must die before he will commit idolatry, murder or adultery" (*The Gospel of John*, vol. 1 [Philadelphia: Westminster, 1956] 1). The woman was not being accused of jaywalking; she was in danger of losing her life.

To make an adultery charge stick, there had to be two witnesses to the act. Not many people commit adultery with two witnesses; usually they are more careful to sin in private. Some commentators therefore believe we are dealing with a case of entrapment: the husband (not mentioned in the text) set up his wife. If this is so, the man wanted to be rid of his wife: her adultery would get him out of the marriage.

Adultery involved a married woman; it was understood in biblical times to be a crime committed *against another man* by sleeping with that man's wife and thus dishonoring him. We are dealing with a woman who was married and unfaithful to her husband. Mosaic Law on adultery was hard and explicit, requiring the deaths of both parties involved (Lev 20:10; Deut 22:22). Death would be by stoning, and the witnesses would be expected to throw the first stone (Deut 17:7).

The real reason the woman was brought before Jesus was not her sin. The scribes and Pharisees were not out to get the woman; they were after Jesus. If Jesus showed sympathy and compassion to the woman, it meant he was soft on the Law of Moses. If he came down hard on her, he was not compassionate to sinners. Brown wrote, "A direct answer by Jesus in the case of the woman would involve him in a legal dispute and put him in trouble with the Romans" (337). At about this time, the Romans had taken the capacity to pronounce a capital sentence away from the Jewish Sanhedrin. Only a Roman trial could sentence someone to death. If Jesus supported Jewish law and came down for the death penalty for the woman, he put himself at risk with the Romans.

Twice our text tells us that Jesus "wrote with his finger on the ground" (8:6, 8). What did he write? We don't know, but there is considerable comment by scholars. Since Jerome (340–420 AD) there has been speculation that Jesus wrote the sins of the woman's accusers. If this is so, it would explain why the accusers melted away when Jesus said, "Let anyone among you who is without sin be the first to throw a stone at her" (8:7). Jerome's answer makes sense, but it is mere speculation.

The case against the woman fell apart when the accusers disappeared. What began as an embarrassing scene ends in restoration. I see four strong teachings you may want to highlight as you interpret the text.

I. Using People

There was meanness and lack of feeling in the scribes and Pharisees who brought the woman to Jesus. They were not out to make a statement for faithfulness in marriage. They were out to put Jesus in a difficult position. The woman was a way to get at Jesus. William Barclay reacted to the callousness of those religious leaders with a scathing statement:

> These Scribes and Pharisees were not looking on this woman as a person at all; they were looking on her only as a thing, an instrument whereby they could formulate a charge against Jesus. They were using her, as a man might use a tool, for their own purposes. To them she had no name, no personality, no heart, no feelings, no emotions; she was simply a pawn in the game whereby they sought to destroy Jesus. (6)

Using people is a treacherous business. If I have an employee, I have hired that person to "use" them. I want some of their time. I want their mind to be in gear while they are at work. I want creativity from them to enlarge my business. I want sensitivity from them when relating to my customers. Literally, for the time they are engaged at my business, I am using them. That's why I hired them. But there are limits to the ways I can use them, and knowing where the boundaries are and respecting those boundaries is the measure of a good manager. People are not widgets to be moved about like inanimate objects. People are made in the image of God and are to be treated with the respect their heavenly Father's image demands.

II. Judging

The Sermon on the Mount has a word from Jesus about judging: "Do not judge, so that you may not be judged. For with the judgment you make you will be judged, and the measure you give will be the measure you get" (Mt 7:1-2). But let me do something I am uncomfortable doing. I'm going to argue that all of us have to make judgments. When I chose a wife, I made a judgment for her and against others. When I was part of the hiring process as pastor of a church, I was making judgments for one and against the other candidates for the job. As administrator of a church staff, I made judgments and reported my observations to the Personnel Committee. When the time came to find new Sunday school teachers, elect new deacons, and choose committee members, I was making small judgments—and I was doing what I was supposed to do.

If what I said in the previous paragraph is true, then Jesus' words in Matthew 7 are pointing us toward a particular kind of judgment. The attitude Jesus wants in us ought to be driven by compassion. Judgment presumes authority over another. The scribes and Pharisees knew Jewish law. Law, when used rightly, is a good thing. Law, when applied without compassion, can be a weapon. Is the rule against adultery a good rule? Yes, but when the rule is broken, how ought we deal with the rule-breaker? And what should be the attitude of the one who sits in judgment?

One possibility is that the rule-breaker be made a public example. In our text, this is what happened to the woman. Her mistake was made widely known. The scribes and Pharisees were upholding the law, but they were destroying a person. The other possibility is sympathy for the rule-breaker. Barclay said, "All true authority is founded on sympathy. When George Whitefield saw the criminal on the way to the gallows, he uttered the famous sentence: 'There, but for the grace of God, go I'" (5).

Good religion is in the business of reclaiming broken people. When religion is used to beat people up, to shame them and destroy self-worth, it is the kind of judgment Jesus condemned.

III. Condoning Sin

Jesus let the woman off pretty easy. The text ends with Jesus saying, "'Woman, where are they? Has no one condemned you?' She said, 'No one, sir.' And Jesus said, 'Neither do I condemn you. Go your way, and from now on do not sin again'" (8:10-11). One could conclude that Jesus did not think adultery was a serious matter, for there is only slight judgment on the woman. Before coming to that conclusion, however, there are two ideas we must keep in mind.

First, the calloused way the scribes and Pharisees treated this poor woman must have pained Jesus. If the religious authorities were putting her down, Jesus was just as diligently trying to give her dignity. He went out of his way to come alongside her. The Jesus attitude toward adultery was laid aside for the sake of the poor wretch who was being trashed before a gawking public. Jesus was against adultery, but he wasn't against the woman who committed it, and he also looked down on such a mean-spirited application of the law. How we apply a rule is as important as the rule.

Second, we must remember that this is not the only thing Jesus ever said on the issue. The clearest example of what Jesus thought of adultery is found in the Sermon on the Mount: "You have heard that it was said, 'You shall not commit adultery.' But I say to you that everyone who looks at a woman with lust has already committed adultery with her in his heart" (Mt 5:27-28). This is not a soft word on adultery. Jesus has made the rule about lust so broad it traps us all. It is one thing to refrain from sinful sexual behavior; it is another thing to keep your mind clean. Jesus raised the standard. He went beyond actions to desire. Jesus was not soft on adultery.

This woman had time to straighten her life, mend her ways, restore her reputation, and live a useful life. Jesus was giving her a second chance to get herself together. Final judgment would come for her as it will come for us all: at the end of time. Judgments in this life are temporary and presume the possibility of restoration. Adultery is always bad, but that sin can be forgiven. There is life beyond adultery, and it can be pure and useful. I suspect Jesus had this in mind when he came down easy on the woman.

IV. Restoring People

I doubt my words can capture the feelings verses 10-11 describe. The woman was "caught in adultery." She was publicly humiliated in the temple: in front of God and everybody. The people who mattered in Jewish society treated her like trash. Jesus was embarrassed by the way the woman was being treated. In a sensitive way, he deflected guilt from the woman and put it on her accusers. It was meant that she should be the villain in this play; but when Jesus redefined the plot, the accusers were the villains.

At last, the words, writings, and attitude of Jesus had made the scribes and Pharisees go away in shame.

Only Jesus and the woman were left. The woman didn't need a sermon against adultery. I suspect she was so sorry for her sins she felt that she could die. At the end of this ugly scene, Jesus spoke to the woman of her future. "From now on do not sin again," he said (8:11). "From now on" meant she had a life to lead, and she could lead it better than she had in the past.

I'm going to interpret what Jesus said to the woman: "The past is past. Let it go; try to get it out of your mind. You have time left; don't commit adultery again. I believe, in spite of what has happened today, that you can be a good person. I'm counting on you, and God bless you." We don't know what became of the woman; I believe she became a believer in Jesus, and I believe she came alongside other women who had committed adultery to minister to them. I believe her bad experience resulted in good.

Notes

Notes

4

HOSPITALITY
TO NEWCOMERS

1 Corinthians 14:20-33a

Central Question

Where should I show more flexibility in my attitudes about worship?

Scripture

1 Corinthians 14:20-33a 20 Brothers and sisters, do not be children in your thinking; rather, be infants in evil, but in thinking be adults. 21 In the law it is written, "By people of strange tongues and by the lips of foreigners I will speak to this people; yet even then they will not listen to me," says the Lord. 22 Tongues, then, are a sign not for believers but for unbelievers, while prophecy is not for unbelievers but for believers. 23 If, therefore, the whole church comes together and all speak in tongues, and outsiders or unbelievers enter, will they not say that you are out of your mind? 24 But if all prophesy, an unbeliever or outsider who enters is reproved by all and called to account by all. 25 After the secrets of the unbeliever's heart are disclosed, that person will bow down before God and worship him, declaring, "God is really among you." 26 What should be done then, my friends? When you come together, each one has a hymn, a lesson, a revelation, a tongue, or an interpretation. Let all things be done for building up. 27 If anyone speaks in a tongue, let there be only two or at most three, and each in turn; and let one interpret. 28 But if there is no one to interpret, let them be silent in church and speak to themselves and to God. 29 Let two or three prophets speak, and let the others weigh what is said. 30 If a revelation is made to someone else sitting nearby, let the first person be silent. 31 For you can all prophesy one by one, so that all may learn and all be encouraged. 32 And the spirits of prophets are subject to the prophets, 33 for God is a God not of disorder but of peace.

Reflecting

Have you ever noticed that places have personalities? Some homes, for example, exude warmth, love, and peace. You can walk into those homes and feel welcomed. Other homes have a cold, distant feel that makes you uncomfortable. Parks, offices, and restaurants have personalities, too. Some of them warm your heart, and some of them leave you cold.

Churches are the same way. Some churches make people feel at home, invite them to stay awhile, and introduce them to the way of faith. Other churches put people off, erect unnecessary barriers, and subtly encourage people to go elsewhere. In other words, some churches are hospitable to newcomers, and some are not.

When the apostle Paul wrote his first letter to the Corinthian Christians, he sensed that their ecclesiastical personality was not hospitable to newcomers. Their freewheeling, let-it-all-hang-out approach to worship was leaving newcomers mystified and excluded. The particular practice of speaking in tongues was making them cold. The Corinthian Christians thought it was wonderful to be so filled with the Spirit that they broke out in ecstatic speech. Paul thought it might be wonderful for them, but not so wonderful for newcomers to their church.

This text is not so much about speaking in tongues as it is about showing hospitality to newcomers and not putting up barriers to people unfamiliar with the Christian Way. As we continue to study missional hospitality, this passage invites us to look at ourselves and our church and see how welcoming we are to newcomers.

Studying

Some Christians in the church in Corinth were speaking in tongues. This phenomenon seems to have been fairly common in the early church. Someone would become so filled with the Spirit that he or she would erupt into ecstatic language. It was not a foreign tongue; it was an unintelligible cry of joy. Unless someone was present to interpret it, the speech edified no one.

Many of us today are baffled by this tongues phenomenon. It isn't anything we've experienced or even have a desire to experience, but it was something people in the early church knew well. It was something Paul himself experienced (see 14:18). But, according to Paul, it was something that could become a barrier for people not versed in Christian ways.

> What religious words do you frequently use that might as well be "speaking in tongues" to a newcomer?

In 1 Corinthians 14, Paul contrasts speaking in tongues and prophesying. By "prophesying," he's not referring to telling the future so much as telling the truth. "Preaching" would be a better way of understanding the word. Paul trumpets the advantages of preaching over tongue-speaking.

Paul states that speaking in tongues makes outsiders nervous: "If, therefore, the whole church comes together and all speak in tongues, and outsiders or unbelievers enter, will they not say that you are out of your mind?" (v. 23). This wild, ecstatic utterance could make newcomers run for the door!

> Have you ever been asked to give up a cherished worship custom? What was the church's rationale for "retiring" this custom?

But, the apostle continues, preaching is intelligible to newcomers and can connect them to God: "But if all prophesy, an unbeliever or outsider who enters is reproved by all and called to account by all. After the secrets of the unbeliever's heart are disclosed, that person will bow down before God and worship him, declaring, 'God is really among you'" (vv. 24-25). In Paul's thinking, preaching is more hospitable and helpful to newcomers than tongue-speaking.

Since that is the case, Paul proceeds to give the Corinthians some practical advice. "What should be done, then, my friends?"

(v. 26) he asks. His answer is built around his desire that they be hospitable to the newcomers among them.

First, Paul says, they should make sure that everything they do in worship builds people up: "Let all things be done for building up" (v. 26). The reason prophecy is better than speaking in tongues is that it has a better chance of building everyone up. Worship is for everyone, not just a select few who happen to have the gift of tongues. That's why one of the key questions we have to ask in our churches is not "What do I like in worship?" but "What will communicate the good news best to the whole group?" Corporate worship is just that: *corporate*. It's not about me, my tastes, or my personal comfort zone. It isn't even about my personal devotional life. Rather, worship is about everyone coming together to worship the God of all of us. That means I might not always be thrilled with every song or sermon.

Second, Paul says, they should make sure that worship is orderly and understandable: "for God is not a God of disorder but of peace" (v. 33). It's not hard to imagine the chaotic scene in the Corinthian worship services. People were jumping to their feet to speak in unknown tongues, sometimes several at a time. Someone else was trying to lead a hymn. Still another was trying to preach a sermon. It was, no doubt, exciting and energizing, but also frenetic and confusing. How could anyone learn anything in that environment? How could anyone hear the still, small voice of God in that chaos?

Paul's counsel was for the Corinthian Christians to remember the uninitiated among them. What would people who wandered in off the street think? What would they learn about Jesus? How could they best be introduced to the Jesus Way?

Most certainly, people wouldn't be introduced to the Jesus Way in an environment of noise and chaos. It would happen in an environment where people tried to meet the needs of others and build others up. It would happen in an environment where the worship was orderly and the message understandable.

What was true for the Corinthians is true for our churches as well. The only way newcomers can come to faith in Christ and have meaningful worship is for us to build them up and speak to them in words they can comprehend. Paul's implied questions to the Corinthians are questions all of our churches need to hear. What about the people who wander in off the street? Will they "get it"? Will our worship leave them wanting more or running for the door?

Understanding

For most of those who are reading this lesson, it is highly probable that the issue that drives newcomers away from our churches is something other than speaking in tongues. That was the issue for the Corinthians, but we have other issues that can make our churches inhospitable to newcomers. For example:

• *Cliques.* We can become so comfortable with our church friends that we unintentionally develop cliques that keep others at bay. We sit beside the same people every Sunday, talk to the same people in Sunday school, and generally enjoy being with the same folks week after week. These are our friends, and we love them! But if we're not careful, discerning newcomers hear our unspoken message loud and clear: "We'll accept you, but you'll never really be one of us."

• *Stained-glass Language.* Newcomers often don't understand our religious lingo. When we start speaking about "redemption," "eschatology," and being "washed in the blood of the Lamb," they smile politely and act like they're having a good time. Then they leave and never come back, preferring to go to a place that doesn't "speak in tongues."

• *Forgetfulness.* Sometimes we forget how hard it is to come into a group as a stranger. That newcomer who walks into the Sunday school class or worship service typically feels alone. Why don't we go over and sit by her? Why don't we escort her to the worship service after Sunday school? Why don't we put ourselves in his shoes and live out the Golden Rule?

• *Rigidity.* Churches have their own distinctive personalities, and each church has developed its own style of worship. But we can grow so rigid that our churches develop personality disorders. We have to sing certain songs a certain way at certain times. The preacher has to say it a certain way to a certain audience in a certain amount of time. Newcomers, not knowing our standard protocol, understandably feel put off by our rigidity. They'd enjoy a little flexibility, but we don't have any to offer.

The principle laid down by Paul in 1 Corinthians 14 is one that applies to all churches in all generations. Hospitality includes being sensitive to the needs of the newcomers who come among us at church. We must be sure that our personality is warm and welcoming.

What About Me?

- *Have I become part of a church clique?* Shutting ourselves off into narrowly defined groups of people we already know and like is easier than we realize. This behavior makes it hard for newcomers to "break in."

- *Do I speak in stained-glass language?* Try to listen to a Sunday school lesson or sermon with the ears of an unchurched person. Pay attention to how many of your favorite hymns and anthems use language people don't understand.

- *Have I forgotten what it's like to be a stranger?* Put yourself in the shoes of the person who has ventured to your church for the first time. He or she knows no one there and is at the mercy of your kindness. Remember how difficult that is and how you would like to be treated in that situation.

- *Can I accept new things in worship?* We all have our likes and dislikes in worship, but have we grown so rigid we can't accept anything new? Remember the seven last words of the church are "we never did it that way before."

HOSPITALITY
TO NEWCOMERS

1 Corinthians 14:20-33

Introduction

Our title is "Hospitality to Newcomers." That means we ought to welcome all kinds of people. That's hard to do. "Newcomers" come in all sizes and cultural tastes. Building a church service that appeals to everyone is nearly impossible. There are young adults who only listen to popular, contemporary music. They want a church service that incorporates their kind of music: electric guitar, drums, and a strong, rhythmic beat. There are also older adults who have come to church all their lives. They learned old hymns when they were children and still like to hear them in church today. They also pay the bills at most churches. Some of these people think guitars and drums are inappropriate in church. Furthermore, most churches have a few trained musicians who have been schooled in Bach, Mozart, and Handel. Some of these people are not the most tolerant sort; they want the music done "right."

So we see church signs that advertise a variety of worship styles, perhaps a "contemporary" service at 9:00 and a "traditional" one at 11:00. That kind of schedule makes an effort to appeal to a wide range of people. There are also churches that try to solve the problem by offering "blended" services that offer a mixture of traditional and contemporary elements (and in my experience leave all parties unsatisfied).

We could resolve this problem if we knew what kind of music God likes; unfortunately, we don't have that information. "Seeker churches" reach for the unchurched with music that sounds a lot like what you hear on the radio. Most mainline churches stick with a more traditional service.

A long time ago, Paul started a new church in Corinth. When Paul left them to preach the gospel elsewhere, the Corinthians made a mess of their worship. Our text comes from one of Paul's letters to the Corinthians. Although our "worship wars" may not involve speaking in tongues, what Paul wrote about worship and attracting "newcomers" is timeless advice.

I. The Corinthian Situation

Paul's letters to the Corinthian Christians look like a grocery list of problems:

• They were new Christians. Most had been pagans with no Jewish tradition to instruct them. None had much of an idea of how to conduct Christian worship.
• Most of them were poor and uneducated (1 Cor 1:26-28). Most of them could not read or write and many of them were slaves. They had no experience in self-governance and no real leaders. The only authority figures were the apostles, and they were either in Jerusalem or traveling about as itinerant preachers.
• They had no tradition to inform them. They had no old patterns to use as models for the present.

The Corinthians had one more problem of such consequence that it needs to be treated separately. They had a group in the church that spoke in tongues. Speaking in tongues is not a problem in most churches. Pentecostals still practice speaking in tongues, but most people who read these words are not familiar with the practice. I've been in church work for a long time, and I've never met anyone who claimed to speak in tongues. The class may need a brief summary of what speaking in tongues entails. William Barclay offers a helpful description in his commentary:

> What happened was this—at a service of the Church someone would fall into an ecstasy and would pour out a torrent of unintelligible sounds in no known language. . . . Sometimes the person so moved could interpret his own outpourings, but

usually it required someone else who had the gift of interpretation to do so. Paul never questioned the reality of the gift of tongues, but he was well aware that it had dangers, for hysteria and ecstasy and a kind of self-hypnotism are very difficult to distinguish. (*The Letters to the Corinthians* [Philadelphia: Westminster, 1956] 124)

To further complicate a difficult situation, the gift of tongues had become a sought-after gift. It was a sign that one was in direct contact with the Holy Spirit. By implication, those who could not speak in tongues were not in close contact with the Spirit. Speaking in tongues was taken as evidence that one was further along in the Christian life than those who could not do so.

Put all the pieces of the Corinthian situation together and you get bedlam. There was no "order of worship." There was no pastor or preacher. There was no tradition that informed how worship ought to be done. It is not surprising that their worship services had become a study in disorder. It was to this situation that Paul wrote three chapters in 1 Corinthians (chs. 12–14).

II. Paul's Corrections

A quick summary of 1 Corinthians 12–14 will put our text in focus. Paul began this way:

(1) There are several spiritual gifts: wisdom, knowledge, faith, healing, miracles, prophecy, discernment, and tongues. All of these gifts are from God (1 Cor 12:4-11).

(2) Paul said the church is like a human body (1 Cor 12:12-31). All the parts are necessary and valuable. When they fit together, all the work of the church will get done. When one part is deemed more valuable than another, confusion and vanity enter the picture.

(3) At this point Paul gives us 1 Corinthians 13, often called "the love chapter." He begins by saying, "If I speak in the tongues of mortals and of angels, but do not have love, I am a noisy gong or

a clanging cymbal" (13:1). In a beautiful and powerful way, Paul told them (and us) that there is nothing more important than loving each other. The Corinthians who were "showing off" by speaking in tongues and claiming a spiritual superiority by it were endangering the fellowship through their lack of love.

(4) In chapter 14, Paul comes to the point.

• When a person is speaking in tongues, he or she is not speaking to the congregation but to God. "Nobody understands them" (14:2), Paul says. The church service is supposed to make sense. If it doesn't, it is wasted time.

• Prophecy is different from speaking in tongues. The effect of prophecy (we would call this preaching) is "upbuilding and encouragement and consolation" (14:3).

• Paul took a swipe at those who spoke in tongues, claiming that they only build up themselves, while prophecy builds up the church (14:4). This is why commentators believe those speaking in tongues were calling attention to themselves.

• Unless there was an interpreter present, there was to be no speaking in tongues. Paul did not disapprove of those who spoke in tongues. On the contrary, he claimed to speak in tongues more than any of them. "Nevertheless," he said, "in church I would rather speak five words with my mind, in order to instruct others also, than ten thousand words in a tongue" (14:18-19). I assume Paul restrained any impulse to speak in tongues when in public and reserved that expression of his spiritual life for privacy.

• Finally, "outsiders or unbelievers" were to be taken into account when the church gathered for worship: "If, therefore, the whole church comes together and all speak in tongues, and outsiders or unbelievers enter, will they not say that you are out of your mind?" (14:23). How could an unbeliever ever determine what the gospel was about if worship was filled with babbling? Church has to make sense to outsiders or they will never come closer to us or to Christ.

III. How Does the Text Speak to Us?

The Corinthians were so caught up in the excitement of being Christians that they went too far. We do not share their context, so interpreting this text will be risky. I am taking their situation and trying to apply it to our different situation.

(1) *There is always tension between thought and feeling.* A good worship experience has some of both, but that's hard to do. Paul is telling the tongues-speakers to give larger place to "prophecy." He is driving them toward a more thoughtful and orderly worship.

If Paul observed our 11:00 worship, what would he say to us? Most of the churches I've observed are thoughtful, orderly, and deliberate. But a lot of them are also dull, boring, and repetitive. If Paul were among us, I suspect he would encourage us to share our feelings, express emotion more freely, and make worship a more joyful experience.

(2) *Pastors and clergy aren't the only people who have something to share in worship.* The Corinthians were doing this part right: "When you come together, each one has a hymn, a lesson, a revelation, a tongue, or an interpretation" (14:26). Anyone could take part in worship, for worship was not confined to what was printed in the bulletin. There was more spontaneity, making room for God's Spirit to break through, and more participation, allowing anyone at worship to speak.

This idea was reborn among the seventeenth-century English Baptists. The first Baptist churches were small. They met in homes, barns, woods, or ships. People sat in a circle, and everyone took part. One would read and interpret a paragraph of Scripture; the others would listen and then comment on what was said. Christopher Hill described Baptist worship in the 1640s this way:

> In the Baptist churches discussion was institutionalized.
> Mrs. Attaway used to call for objections after her sermons, "for
> it was their custom to give liberty in that kind." Henry Denne
> had a similar practice. At the Bell Alley Baptist church public
> debates were held at which all might voice their opinions. It was

a rule among General Baptists "that it shall be lawful for any person to improve their gifts in the presence of the congregation." (*The World Turned Upside Down, Radical Ideas During the English Revolution* [London: Penguin, 1991] 105)

This idea was laid aside because some people abused it, but in our text Paul leaves the door open for any layperson to speak their mind in worship. God is not confined to the insights of a pastor, nor is the Holy Spirit locked onto the railroad track of an "order of worship." The text is telling us to let a little fresh air into our worship. Open the door for more lay participation. The Corinthians were too loose, but we are too tight. There has to be a middle way.

(3) *Take "outsiders or unbelievers" into account when planning worship.* Paul was concerned to attract new people to Christ. He was always thinking about what "newcomers" were thinking. Does our worship attract? Or is our worship predictable? Does it use language only church people can understand? Paul was making a case for commonsense worship that would grab the attention of "newcomers" and draw them back for more.

In our day we have "seeker churches." These churches are dedicated to getting a hearing for the gospel with people who have not been going to church. Nearly all these churches are "contemporary" in style. I don't go to that kind of church, but I'm glad those churches are out there and I want them to succeed. They are doing something most of us are not doing well: attracting "newcomers." We ought not criticize them.

Can a "seeker church" go too far? Can it be more about entertainment than content, more about display than substance? I'm sure that has happened, but that's not the problem most of our churches have. We have shut out laypeople from meaningful participation in the service. We have scheduled the order of worship as if it were written in stone. Too many preachers can't preach in an interesting way. The effect of this pattern of dull predictability is that our churches have few "newcomers." We have designed a service that has run them off, and we have no one to blame but ourselves.

Notes

Notes

5

HOSPITALITY TO CHRIST

Matthew 25:31-46

Central Question

What does my hospitality say about my relationship with Christ?

Scripture

Matthew 25:31-46 31 "When the Son of Man comes in his glory, and all the angels with him, then he will sit on the throne of his glory. 32 All the nations will be gathered before him, and he will separate people one from another as a shepherd separates the sheep from the goats, 33 and he will put the sheep at his right hand and the goats at the left. 34 Then the king will say to those at his right hand, 'Come, you that are blessed by my Father, inherit the kingdom prepared for you from the foundation of the world; 35 for I was hungry and you gave me food, I was thirsty and you gave me something to drink, I was a stranger and you welcomed me, 36 I was naked and you gave me clothing, I was sick and you took care of me, I was in prison and you visited me.' 37 Then the righteous will answer him, 'Lord, when was it that we saw you hungry and gave you food, or thirsty and gave you something to drink? 38 And when was it that we saw you a stranger and welcomed you, or naked and gave you clothing? 39 And when was it that we saw you sick or in prison and visited you?' 40 And the king will answer them, 'Truly I tell you, just as you did it to one of the least of these who are members of my family, you did it to me.' 41 Then he will say to those at his left hand, 'You that are accursed, depart from me into the eternal fire prepared for the devil and his angels; 42 for I was hungry and you gave me no food, I was thirsty and you gave me nothing to drink, 43 I was a stranger and you did not welcome me, naked and you did not give me clothing, sick and in prison and you did not visit me.' 44 Then they also will answer, 'Lord, when was it that we saw you hungry or thirsty or a stranger or naked or sick or in prison, and did not take care of you?' 45 Then he will answer them, 'Truly I tell you, just as you did not do it to one of the least of these, you did not do it to me.' 46 And these will go away into eternal punishment, but the righteous into eternal life."

Reflecting

As I write this, my wife and I are eagerly awaiting the arrival of our first grandchild. Anthony Judson Edwards is scheduled to make his public debut sometime next month. We have been following his prenatal development with great interest. We get an online report each week telling us how big he is, what is happening in his body, and what new skills he's acquiring. It's been exciting to follow his progress in the womb and to dream of the day he will be born.

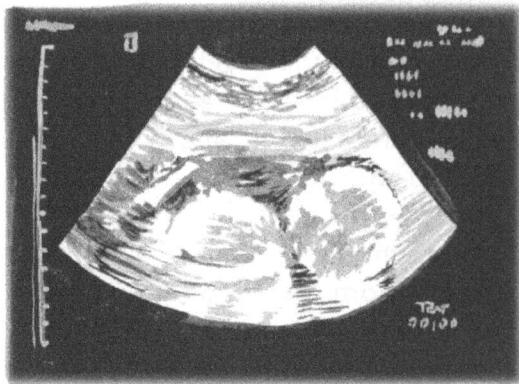

This process has reminded me again of the wonder and miracle of birth. It has reminded me of David's words in Psalm 139:13-14: "For it was you who formed my inward parts; you knit me together in my mother's womb. I praise you, for I am fearfully and wonderfully made." It has also reminded me that *every person* is a miracle, not just my grandson-to-be. Every person is a thought of God, a one-of-a-kind creation. And every person deserves to be treated as the miracle that he or she is.

Our final session in this unit on "missional hospitality" is built around Jesus' parable of the sheep and the goats. This parable underscores the

> When have you "met Jesus" while helping another? How did you become aware of Jesus' presence?

same truth my grandson-to-be has been teaching me: every person is a miracle, "fearfully and wonderfully made" by God. In this parable, Jesus reminds us that the hungry, the thirsty, the stranger, the naked, the sick, and the prisoner are all worthy of our attention and love. All of "the least of these" are thoughts of God, and, in showing hospitality to them, we also show hospitality to Christ.

Studying

In Matthew's Gospel, this story of the sheep and the goats is the last story Jesus tells before the events surrounding his arrest and crucifixion start to unfold. Right after this story, we begin to hear about Judas, Gethsemane, and Peter denying Jesus three times. It is fair to assume that, except for his words at the Last Supper, this story is the final thing Jesus taught before he died. Ben Witherington notes,

> Appropriately enough, the last discourse material in Matthew is a story about final judgment. This story is unique to this Gospel and rounds out all of the Matthean Gospel on a clearly eschatological note. There can be little doubt that this Evangelist has not traded in Jesus' future eschatology for more emphasis on the present eschatological situation, unlike what seems to be the case in Luke's Gospel. A good case can be made that we should not see this as a parable but rather as an apocalyptic prophecy with some parabolic elements. This is only appropriate for an apocalyptic sage like Jesus. (465)

Jesus' final discourse is a simple story of the final judgment. "All the nations will be gathered before him," he says, "and he will separate people one from another as a shepherd separates the sheep from the goats" (v. 32). The sheep are put at Jesus' right hand and welcomed because they took care of the hungry, the thirsty, the stranger, the

Structurally what is striking about this passage is the fourfold repetition of the list of needs, always in this order: hungry, thirsty, stranger, naked, sick, and in prison. This presents a short list of tasks that the true disciple is to be about until the Son of Man returns. (Witherington, 466)

naked, the sick, and the prisoner. The goats are placed at his left hand and condemned because they didn't take care of these people. As the story unfolds, three things become crystal clear.

First, *the basis of the judgment is not "big things," but "little things."* It seems that the sheep didn't do anything monumentally generous. Giving a morsel of food to a hungry person or a drink of water to a thirsty person is not exactly headline material. So, too, it seems that the goats didn't do anything awful. They didn't murder, steal, or commit adultery; they simply failed to see—or respond to—"the least of these." One of the obvious points of the story is that Jesus wants his followers to take hold of "the near edge" of problems and make a difference right there. His people don't necessarily make headlines, but they are sensitive to the needs of the people around them. They do have open hands, open hearts, and open homes. They do practice hospitality as a normal way of life.

Second, *the righteous ones are in no way trying to earn a reward.* When the king welcomes those on his right hand, they are surprised. They even ask him as to their qualifications. It's as if they are asking, "What did we ever do to merit sheep status and eternal life?" They weren't working for a reward; they were just going about life with an attitude of servanthood and hospitality. There is a kind of piety that toots its own horn and seeks applause, but Jesus consistently urged his followers to run away from that kind of religion. That was the piety of the scribes and Pharisees. He wanted his followers to work quietly behind the scenes, taking care of "the least of these." It is interesting to note, too, that the goats were clueless as to why they were condemned. They didn't know it was so vital to show hospitality to the hurting.

Third, *taking care of "the least of these" is really taking care of Jesus.* The sheep hear the good news that their ministry to the needy was ministry to Jesus himself. And the goats hear the bad news that their neglect of the needy was really neglect of Jesus. Who knew that hungry person was Jesus in disguise? Who knew that sick, old woman was Jesus incognito? One of the ways we grow to see every person as a miracle and a thought of God is to remember this truth: Jesus hides in strange places and unsuspecting people, and every hurting person we meet gives us the opportunity to meet him.

One of the things we have to remember when we try to interpret a story like this one is that we must read it alongside the rest of the New Testament. If we pull this parable out and let it stand alone, we might conclude that all anyone has to do to be a "sheep" and get eternal life is to be hospitable to "the least of these." Standing alone, this story could lead us to the notion of salvation by works. Just be kind to the needy, and you get eternal life.

But placed alongside passages like John 3:16 and Ephesians 2:8-9, this story shapes and refines our faith. Yes, we are saved by believing in Jesus, as John 3:16 tells us. Yes, we are saved by grace through faith, not of works, as Ephesians 2:8-9 tells us. But any true follower of Jesus is changed by that encounter. And any true follower of Jesus sees people who are hurting and tries to help them. The point of the story is that Jesus' people naturally respond to "the least of these" and, in doing so, are showing hospitality to Jesus himself.

Understanding

When my children were in high school, they both participated in sports. I had a daily routine of waking up early and racing to the front yard to retrieve the morning paper. I always turned first to the sports page to see if one of my children was listed as high scorer in the basketball game or one of the leading receivers in the football statistics. If they made the paper, it made my day.

Any parent knows about that. What happens to our children profoundly affects us. When they get honored, we swell with pride. When they suffer disgrace, we do too. We are so connected to our offspring that we feel what they feel. Inasmuch as you do it to them, you do it to us.

In the parable of the sheep and goats, Jesus wants us to remember that suffering people are God's children, people of immeasurable worth. When they hurt, God hurts. When they are helped, God is helped. God cares so profoundly for "the least of these" that Jesus could say, "Just as you did it to one of the least of these who are members of my family, you did it to me" (v. 40).

Those of us who have pledged our allegiance to Jesus want to do everything possible to show him our love. That means we will worship, pray, study Scripture, and share his way with our friends. But this parable tells us another way we make our love for Jesus known: we care for the hungry, the thirsty, the stranger, the naked, the sick, and the prisoner. When we show hospitality to them, we show hospitality to Jesus.

What About Me?

• *Little things matter.* What Jesus calls us to do in this parable seems almost too easy. Give a meal to a hungry person and a cup of water to one who is thirsty. Make a stranger feel welcome and give clothes to a needy person. Visit someone who is sick or in prison. Evidently, those little things matter a lot to him. He calls us not to make headlines but to take hold of the near edge of some problem.

• *Some of the best ministry we ever do will be unintentional.* That is, we will not think about it. It will just come from a life that sees and notices people who have a need. We will not even be aware we are doing something special.

• *We enter into a relationship with God by simply accepting God's grace.* But once we enter into that relationship, we begin to change. We have our eyes opened to the people around us, and we begin to care about them. We're saved by grace, but that grace makes us attentive to "the least of these."

• *Hospitality is a key component of following Jesus.* This parable finishes our study of "missional hospitality." In previous sessions, we've seen that we are to show hospitality to strangers, the poor, sinners, and newcomers. As we open our hearts and resources to these people, we are showing hospitality to Jesus himself.

Resource

Colin Morris, *Include Me Out! Confessions of an Ecclesiastical Coward* (New York: Fontana, 1975).

Ben Witherington III, *Matthew*, Smyth & Helwys Bible Commentary (Macon GA: Smyth & Helwys, 2006).

HOSPITALITY TO CHRIST

Matthew 25:31-46

Introduction

Eugene Boring began his comment on our text saying, "These are the last words of Jesus' last discourse, a climactic point to which Matthew has carefully built" ("Matthew," *The New Interpreter's Bible*, vol. 8 [Nashville: Abingdon, 1995] 455). According to Frank Stagg, "This passage unmistakably goes back to Jesus and preserves some of the deepest and most far-reaching teaching" ("Matthew," *The Broadman Bible Commentary*, vol. 8 [Nashville: Broadman, 1969] 226).

Most of us have been taught that the way to go to heaven is "to believe in Jesus." This is what the Bible says, but there is more. The problem with what we have been taught is not that it is not true; the problem is that it is not the whole truth. In Matthew, Mark, and Luke there is frequently an implied teaching that says we have to "do something" to win God's final approval at the last judgment; our text specifically says we have to "do something."

In the New Testament there are two ways outlined to go to heaven:

(1) Salvation is ours by believing in Jesus. Paul wanted to make the point that works, done with a view toward earning salvation, would not get us to heaven. Reformation theology emphasized God's grace: salvation is a gift. We do not work to earn it. There is much biblical support for this position, and our lesson does not contradict it. Stagg said, "Although ministry to the needs of other people is unmistakably the criterion of judgment emphasized here, Jesus' omission of other demands does not exclude them" (227).

(2) Our text offers a second salvation formula: People who have responded to human need as a life pattern have actually been

responding to Christ. To help the poor and helpless is to help Christ. These people have won God's final approval and will "inherit the kingdom prepared for you from the foundation of the world" (25:34).

There have been times when I've been perplexed by the two salvation standards, but at this point in my life any difference between them troubles me no longer. I have blended them together. I believe in Jesus in order to be a Christian, *and* I believe I must respond to the poor as our text teaches if I want to go to heaven. It seems to me no one has put the two ideas together better than James, who said, "What good is it, my brothers and sisters, if you say you have faith but do not have works? Can faith save you? If a brother or sister is naked and lacks daily food, and one of you says to them, 'Go in peace; keep warm and eat your fill,' and yet you do not supply their bodily needs, what is the good of that? So faith by itself, if it has no works, is dead" (Jas 2:14-17).

Obviously, we are dealing with an old dispute. If it goes back to James, it must have been present in the earliest days of the church. I have come to hold both opinions. I have to "believe" (as John and Paul taught), and I have to respond to the poor and helpless (as in Matthew, Luke, and James). The people who try to reduce this discussion to "either-or" are the ones who do harm.

I. Standards for Last Judgment are Simple, Physical, and Concrete

Jesus told a story that gives us a picture of the way all of us will stand for our final examination.

(1) Jesus is the "Son of Man" (Mt 25:31), the one who was questioned, taunted, badgered, pestered, betrayed, abused at trial, and crucified. Jesus will "come in his glory, and all his angels with him" (25:31). God has exalted him; he will preside over judgment (Phil 2:11).

(2) "All the nations will be gathered before him" (Mt 25:32). No one will be exempt from judgment. When the Master returns, we must give an account.

(3) Jesus will separate the sheep from the goats, the people who are acceptable to God from those who are not. Jesus said the separation would be like a shepherd who customarily keeps his flock of sheep and goats together until evening, when he divides them. Sheep in that time and region were white, but goats were black. The shepherd had no problem distinguishing between them.

(4) The standard for judgment is the point of the story. In this text there is no theological language. No one will be asked to confess faith in Jesus. Nothing is said about "grace, justification, or the forgiveness of sins. What counts is whether one has acted with loving care for needy people" (Boring, 455). This is the main point of the lesson, and no other teaching should obscure it.

There have been times when I fretted about the fairness of God's final judgment. What about the people who never had a chance to hear about Jesus? What about people who lived before Jesus? What about people who listened to preachers like me and were confused about what God expected of them? The standard Jesus outlines in our text is simple, direct, and easy to understand. William Barclay said, "The things which Jesus picks out—giving a hungry man a meal, or a thirsty man a drink, welcoming a stranger, cheering the sick, visiting the prisoner—are things which anyone can do.... It is a case of giving simple, human help to the people we meet every day" (*The Gospel of Matthew*, vol. 2 [Philadelphia: Westminster, 1958] 359). This is a gospel anyone can understand.

This lesson is not the sum of the New Testament, and it ought not be taught as if it were. We don't need to deny grace and forgiveness. They have their place. But the correcting balance this text offers our theology is understated. We need to put today's teaching alongside grace, faith, and forgiveness more often than we do.

II. The Surprises Are the Disturbing Part of this Text

The first surprise comes to the "sheep," the righteous. Jesus said they were to "inherit the kingdom prepared for you from the foundation of the world" (25:34). Jesus personalized the little kindnesses of the righteous: "I was hungry and you gave me food, I was thirsty and you gave me something to drink, I was a stranger and you welcomed me, I was naked and you gave me clothing, I was sick and you took care of me, I was in prison and you visited me" (25:35-36). Jesus redirected the kindnesses; they weren't done for the nameless poor. They were done for him.

What Jesus said surprised the righteous. They asked, "Lord, when was it that we saw you hungry and gave you food?" (25:37-39). This tells us that the small kindnesses of the righteous were uncalculating. Their good deeds, done over the course of a life-time, were not part of a scheme to get to heaven. They were the natural responses of compassionate people doing the right thing as opportunity arose. Frank Stagg put it this way: "They were not religious acts calculated to be good, to please God, or to gain reward. They were the spontaneous acts, their normal response to another human being in need" (227).

The second surprise came from the other group, the goats. When told they were not acceptable to God because they had withheld small kindnesses from the poor—and thus from Jesus—they were aghast! They asked, "Lord, when was it that we saw you hungry or thirsty or a stranger or naked or sick or in prison, and did not take care of you?" (25:44). If the poor wore a sign that dangled from their necks that said, "I am Jesus," we might be more caring of them. But the needy often smell bad, have marginal manners, are sometimes lazy, and usually are confined to a part of town where we rarely see them. They are easy to miss.

Could some of the condemned in this story be church people? That's the part that troubles me. I could be completely orthodox theologically and wind up in the wrong group on Judgment Day. Not enough of our church budgets are directed to the simple care of the needy. Not enough of my private treasure is directed toward them, either. Our text leaves my eternal destination in question because of it. I don't think church rolls will have much to do with who goes to heaven, but little kindnesses will.

III. To Respond to the Helpless Is to Care for Jesus

In this text Jesus is identified in two ways. First, he is called "the Son of Man," "the king," and "Lord." No longer is Jesus to be viewed as a servant, scorned or rejected; in this teaching he returns as the one who presides over final judgment. He speaks the judgment of God on all humanity. Some have used this text to justify a kind of Christless humanitarianism. They argue, "never mind Christ; take care of the poor." Taking care of the poor is one of the main teachings in the text, but nothing can obscure the large place given to Jesus in this passage, the Bible's best picture of the last judgment. To leave Jesus and Christology out of this text is to rewrite the story in ways that are forbidden to an honest interpreter.

Second, Jesus is closely identified with the poor. The text says that when we help the hungry, the naked, the sick, and the imprisoned, we are helping Christ himself (v. 40). The "family of God" includes people who are at the margins of polite society, and Jesus went out of his way to see to it that those marginal people were included.

The inclusion of the poor in the family of God is clear and repetitious in the Bible. The Law of Moses gave the poor special attention. The prophets often chided Israel for failing to care for the poor. Jesus was a friend of the poor and outcast. Paul said the Corinthian church was made up of nobodies, slaves, and poor (1 Cor 1:26-29). James spoke for inclusion of the poor (Jas 2:1-7; 5:1-6). The pattern of the Bible is only underscored in this text. What Jesus did in coming alongside the poor is in harmony with the rest of Scripture.

IV. God Condemns No One; Our Response to Need Is Our Judgment

Our text does not make Jesus a stern judge. All Jesus does is read the record.

Perhaps we might imagine that somewhere in God's eternal bookkeeping department there is an angel. That angel is much like a court recorder; all the angel does is record my responses to human need throughout my lifetime. At judgment the books are opened, and my record determines my judgment. God did not consign me to hell by some predetermined system of theology. God did not send me to hell because he was in a bad humor or was "out to get me." If I understand the nature of God, God was watching in heaven, pulling for me to do the right thing day after day. He was allowing me to make the decision, but he was pulling for me to do the right thing.

God has made a rule and will not break it. I can choose to do the caring thing or I can choose to ignore the poor. What happens to me at judgment is not God's doing. The record I have written throughout my life determines my judgment. That is the sense of our lesson, and it is the clearest picture of last judgment given in the entire Bible.

Sometimes a study of theology confuses more than it helps. There is a simplicity and fairness in this text that puts to rest most of my theological questions. Even pagans who have been kept from any knowledge of Jesus have the door to heaven opened for them in this teaching. One text does not capture all the Bible has to say on any subject, but this one surely puts judgment in a different light.

Notes

Notes

nextsunday
STUDIES

1 Peter
Keep Hope Alive

This study of First Peter focuses on keeping hope alive in the face of pressures and circumstances that could possibly extinguish it completely, or worse, turn authentic faith into a pale replica of the real thing.

Apocalyptic Literature

This study examines five apocalyptic texts in the Bible—from Zechariah, Daniel, Matthew, and Revelation. With each new year bringing a new prediction of impending doom, it is always a perfect time to get the story straight. Apocalyptic literature does not address the future. It addresses our present.

Approaching a Missional Mindset

The World isn't the same as it once was. We must be the church in a new place, in unimagined ways, and with a wider range of people. Engage your small group with the radical and refreshing challenge of developing a "missional lifestyle."

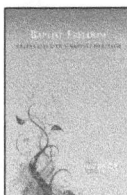

Baptist Freedom
Celebrating Our Baptist Heritage

What makes a Baptist a Baptist? Of course, the ultimate answer is simple: membership in a local Baptist church. But there are all kinds of Baptist churches! What are the spiritual and theological marks of a Baptist? What is the shape and the feel of Baptist Christianity?

The Bible and the Arts

God has used artistic expression throughout the centuries to convey truth, offer blessing, and urge believers to deeper faithfulness. In modern life, artistic expression flourishes, from movies to books to music to paintings to photographs. Sometimes artists are intentional about trying to portray God's truths. Other times, perhaps God is working even when the artist is unaware of it. As believers, we may hear and see God at work in many art forms.

Challenges of the Christian Life

The way of the cross is difficult, and taking Jesus seriously means looking honestly at how we fall short of God's best hopes for us and seeing how much we need God's grace. For all of us there are times when we need to remember that Christ is our saving grace and recommit ourselves to the journey of faith, rediscovering, again and again, the life-giving purpose described in the book of Ephesians.

Christ Is Born!

Even in the midst of difficult circumstances, Advent is a time when we can find hope. Much like today, people in the 1st century church faced struggles. Examining the Gospel of Matthew, lessons include "Waiting for Christ," "Preparing for Christ," "Expecting Christ," "Announcing Christ," and "The Arrival of Christ."

Christians and Hunger

These sessions challenge us to apply gospel lenses and holy imagination to what literally gives us energy to live: food. With God's grace, we have the opportunity to imagine communities where tables are large and all are fed.

Christmas in Mark

In the early chapters of Mark, we will encounter a Christmas story. This story, however, will not be quite like the one told by other Gospel writers, but it will resonate with the reality of your life. Mark doesn't deny the beauty or reality of the nativity; however, he seems to believe that Christmas begins—the gospel begins—when Christ intrudes upon the hard realities of life.

The Church on a Mission

What does it mean to be a church on a mission? The lesson of Acts 1:8 is that we must simultaneously carry out Christ's mandate at home, in our region, in places that have been our blind spots, and around the world.

Colossians
Living the Faith Faithfully

Paul's letter to the Colossians begins with a high-minded philosophical defense of the faith, but concludes with a collection of extremely practical advice for living by faith. This study addresses the questions many Christians face today, helping them apply Paul's practical advice in their own lives.

Easter Confessions

Easter confession is often found on many different lips in the Gospel of John. When we listen carefully, those ancient confessions still echo into this new millennium.

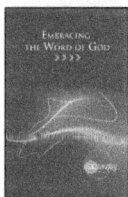

Embracing the Word of God

We live during a time of transition in Christian history. Basic assumptions about the truth of the Christian faith are being questioned, not only by nonbelievers, but by Christians themselves. First John offers a starting point for understanding of what it means to "be" Christian.

Esther: A Woman of Discretion and Valor

The book of Esther is not a record of historical facts as such. Rather, it is a magnificent narrative that refuses to interpret life as being driven by coincidence or happenstance. In the otherwise unknown characters of Esther, Haman, and Mordecai, we trace the movement of the divine hand as God collaborates with God's risk-taking people to rescue them from the hand of their enemies.

Facing Life's Challenges

This study explores four significant challenges common to most persons of faith: the challenge of new light, the challenge of time's limit, the challenge of living with mystery, and the challenge of authentic spirituality. Although these issues are neither simple nor easy to ponder, this study effectively leads us in confronting these challenges.

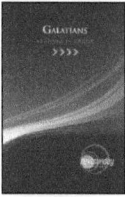

Galatians
Freedom in Christ

Paul wrote with fiery passion, as you will notice from the opening paragraphs of this letter to the Galatians. But his language reveals that he was writing about a crucially important issue—the very nature of salvation in Christ.

A Holy and Surprising Birth

Christmas begins here—discover these five love stories from the book of Luke and renew your appreciation of God's laborious effort to birth our salvation.

How Does the Church Decide?

An array of decisions draw energy and time from church members. These decisions may be theological, such as mode of baptism, aesthetic, such as the color of the sanctuary carpet, or functional, such as the selection of a new minister. This study will consider how the church has made its decisions in the past to help guide our decisions today.

Is God Calling?

Witness the varying forms of God's call, the variety of people called, and the variety of responses. Perhaps God's call to you will become clearer.

James
Gaining True Wisdom

If we'll be honest with God and ourselves as we study what James says, we can make great strides toward wisdom and a living faith.

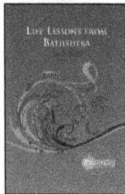

Life Lessons from Bathsheba

Who was Bathsheba? She was a complex figure who developed from the silent object of David's lust into a powerful, vocal, and influential queen mother.

Life Lessons from David

In the Bible, we catch David in the various stages of the human journey: childhood, adolescence, adulthood, and senior adulthood. From the biblical treatment of the stages of David's life, we can land some insights to assist us in better understanding the human journey.

The Matriarchs

The matriarchs of Genesis offer their lives as a testimony of faith, perseverance, and audacity. We learn from their mistakes and suffering. We will gain the hope of Hagar, the joy of Sarah, and the audacity of Rebekah as we are challenged to examine our prejudices and our insecurities while studying Esau and Jacob's wives.

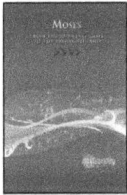

Moses
From the Burning Bush to the Promised Land

We would do well to trace the life of Moses so we might discover how his life changed, both personally and as Israel's leader, as he learned what it meant to love God with all his heart, soul, and strength.

Old Testament Promises to God

Some individuals may feel that our promises couldn't possibly mean anything to God. Perhaps the real question is this: under what circumstances should or do we make such promises? The Old Testament contains several examples of people making promises to God, using the unique form of a biblical "vow."

The Passion of Christ

The four lessons in this unit highlight the faith struggles of the early disciples. In lesson one, Jesus addresses the issues of faith and practice. In lesson two, we meet Judas who, like us, struggled with God's Kingdom and human kingdoms. In lesson three, the issue of temptation reminds us that our faith journey is a constant challenge. Lesson Four invites us to remember Peter's experience of "faith failure." Peter's failure, however, is not the final word. There is forgiveness.

The Prayer Life of Jesus

The study of Jesus' prayer life can deepen our own prayer practices. These five sessions examine the importance of prayer at various stages of Jesus' life and ministry. He made no important decisions without consulting God.

Proverbs for Living

Long ago, a collection of wise teachers committed themselves to the ways of God and collected this wisdom into what we know as the book of Proverbs. These four lessons explore the simple truth of Proverbs: there is a good life to be had—a life lived in faithfulness to God.

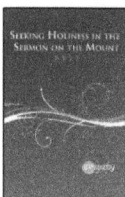

Seeking Holiness in the Sermon on the Mount

The Sermon on the Mount has long been recognized as the pinnacle of Jesus' teaching. But with this importance in mind, it's easy to think of Jesus' teachings as lofty and idealistic, offering little guidance for everyday life. Perhaps Jesus' sermon allows us to see beyond ourselves, beyond our own failures and shortcomings—revealing God's intention for our lives.

Spiritual Disciplines
Obligation or Opportunity?

The spiritual disciplines help deepen a believer's faith and increases his or her intimacy with Christ. In this study, we take a deeper look at some of the disciplines and consider their practice as a response to God's love.

Stewardship
A Way of Living

Great News! Stewardship is not about money! At least not *just* about money. Certainly, stewardship relates to money, and, yes, we need to tithe. However, stewardship branches out into multiple areas of life. Properly practiced, this act of service can lead to peace and purpose in living.

The Ten Commandments

When the Ten Commandments are in the news, it is usually because a judge or teacher has hung them up on the walls. The Ten Commandments do not need to be posted or even preached nearly so much as they need to be practiced and viewed as life-giving, joyful affirmations of a better way of life.

What Would Jesus Say?
A Lenten Study

To address what Jesus would say, we need to discover what Jesus did say. These lessons will attempt to help us understand Jesus' teachings and apply them today.

**NextSunday Studies
are available from**

NextSunday
Resources

www.ingramcontent.com/pod-product-compliance
Lightning Source LLC
Chambersburg PA
CBHW070550030426
42337CB00016B/2426